This Marvellous Terrible Place

This Marvellous Terrible Place

Images of Newfoundland and Labrador

Yva Momatiuk and John Eastcott

Camden House

© Copyright 1988 by Yva Momatiuk and John Eastcott

Canadian Cataloguing in Publication Data

Momatiuk, Yva, 1940-
    This marvellous terrible place

ISBN 0-920656-67-6

1. Newfoundland—Social life and customs.
2. Newfoundland—Description and travel—Views.
I. Eastcott, John, 1952-   . II. Title.

FC2168.M65 1988   971.8   C88-094515-X
F1122.M65 1988

Trade distribution by
Firefly Books
3520 Pharmacy Avenue, Unit 1-C
Scarborough, Ontario
Canada M1W 2T8

Printed in Canada for
Camden House Publishing
(a division of Telemedia Publishing Inc.)
7 Queen Victoria Road
Camden East, Ontario
K0K 1J0

Designed by
Linda J. Menyes

Colour separations by
Hadwen Graphics Limited
Ottawa, Ontario

Printed and bound in Canada by
D.W. Friesen & Sons Ltd.
Altona, Manitoba

Printed on 80-lb. Jensen Gloss

Front Cover: Storm, François

Sunset over Hermitage Bay

To Tara, who spent her second birthday in the Torngats, her fourth in Conception Bay and her eighth in northern Bonavista Bay.

Acknowledgements

Bay de Verde, Conception Bay

We are deeply indebted to the people of Newfoundland and Labrador who trusted us with their stories, who nurtured us when we were tired and hungry and whose passion for living kept our inspiration alive.

Our debt of gratitude is also to those who helped us formulate ideas and gave us direction: Ann Bell, Reg and Tom Best, Eric Blundon, Patricia Grattan, David Huddlestone, Donald Hustins, Marilyn John, Andy Jones, Pamela Karasek, Margaret Kearny, Laurie Locke, Colleen Lynch, Judy McGrath, Elliott Merrick, Anstiss Morrill, Al Pittman, Bill Ritchie and Joseph Smallwood. We also thank Sam Anderson, Roger and Sheri Baird, Tim Borlase, Maud Chaulk, Jean Crane, Marnie and Blake Cryderman, Ada and Clayton Dally, Stuart Fairhurst, Hayward Groves, Jacquie Hunter, Laura and Lawrence Jackson, Rebecca Jamieson, Wayne Jenkins, Al Klevoric, Alfreda and Ron Lethbridge, Chesley Lethbridge, Kurt Mahle, Irene McGuire, Patrick Nagle, Eva Nochesak, Sadie Popovitch-Penny, Matthew Rich, Gerald Riggs, James Roche, Shauna Steffla, the late Annie Walters, Katherine Walters and David Zelcer.

Several scientists and scholars lent their critical thinking to our ideas. We particularly thank Peter Beamish, Carol Brice-Bennett, David Buchan, Louis Chiaramonte, Herbert Halpert, Ruth McLagan, David Nettleship, Deannie Renouf, George Story, Adrian Tanner, Jane Sproull Thomson and Callum Thomson.

For their forever open doors, invaluable advice and willingness to give so much of themselves, we are indebted to Jon and Judy Lien, Pat McLeod, William and Janet Montevecchi, Johanna and John Terriak, Jack and Florence Troake, Gisela Westphalen and Tony Williamson.

We are thankful to David Quinton for his guidance and inspiration, to Reginald and Melita Prosser for their aid in difficult moments, to Clyde and Terry House for their generosity and for our visit to their Hunt River camp, to David Brown for his friendship and for our Torngat days together, to John and Joyce Michelin for their hospitality, to Doris Saunders for her selfless help, to Joshua Marsden for his enlightening letters, to Stu Luttich for caribou talks and much advice, to Jane Hutchins for her encouragement and enthusiasm, to Billy Snook for Salmon River walks, to Clyde Rose for his books and songs, to Horace Goudie for our days in Labrador, to Gilbert Higgins for his library and the research and to Paula Arnet and Joanna Gerwel who were, at different times, our travelling companions.

For two Yuletides of cheer and giving, we are grateful to everyone in the Newfoundland outport of François, especially Lewis and Doris Andrews, Mary and Walter Andrews, Harvey Baggs, Kathleen Courtney, Clyde Durnford, Evelyn Durnford, Gordon and Maud Durnford, Reginald and Minnie Durnford, Roland Durnford, Ruth and Riley Durnford, George and Doris Fudge, Ron and Linda Fudge, Annie and Lloyd Greene, Gladys and Stuart Marsden, the late John Priddle, Nelson Priddle, Eli and Shirley Skinner, Mary Ann Skinner and the late Robert Skinner.

We are most appreciative of the help rendered by the institutions and publishers that assisted us in our extensive and often difficult fieldwork. The National Geographic Society twice sponsored and generously supported our work in the province, and Robert Gilka, Thomas Powell III and Robert Patton provided us with much encouragement. *Equinox* magazine also sent us to Newfoundland twice, with Bart Robinson and Barry Estabrook helping us shape our coverage. Gros Morne National Park's staff and its superintendent, Don Lockwood, gave us excellent logistic support. Kirk Smith of Canada's Sealers Association supplied us with information and guidance. The officers of the Department of Fisheries and Oceans in Twillingate offered their opinions and room on their boats. Sealand Helicopters manipulated schedules to accommodate our needs. Petro-Canada Inc., especially Ken MacDonald and the late Brian Garbett, were instrumental in helping us to reach our destinations in Labrador—and to return safely.

We would like to express much gratitude to our publisher, Frank B. Edwards, to our editors, Tracy C. Read and Merilyn Mohr, to art director Linda Menyes and to Jill Walker and Patricia Denard-Hinch for their enthusiasm and words of encouragement and advice.

Finally, we would like to give the warmest thanks to our daughter, Tara, who shared every step with us.

Eclipse Harbour, Torngat Mountains

After seven years of intermittent visits to Newfoundland and Labrador, photojournalists Yva Momatiuk and John Eastcott have come to know the region and its inhabitants as well as any outsiders could. The couple first visited the province in 1981, on assignment for the National Geographic Society. Immediately struck by the rugged beauty of the area and the harsh realities of life there, Yva and John soon became fascinated by the ties that bind the local people to the land, the sea—and one another.

"It is an uneasy bond," they wrote in a note to their editors during the preparation of *This Marvellous Terrible Place*, "one born of old hardships, fractured by recent social and economic changes and by the erosion of community life that once sustained the people through the leanest of years." Uneasy or not, to the visitors, the bond still seemed incredibly strong—an anachronism of sorts in an age of mobility and constant change. Again and again, the pair were drawn back to the barrens and the outports, determined to record in words and pictures the spirit of an uncommon people.

"We are just observers," says Yva. "In an age which is cynical about the forces that push mankind, the wild country fills us with wonderment, with enthusiasm and with faith."

Their common struggle against the elements has made the people of Labrador and Newfoundland a tenacious lot, drawn together for centuries out of necessity but still fiercely independent—occasionally of one another, more often of the rest of the world. Typically, despite the incursion of the mass media, Newfoundlanders speak in a language that at times seems almost foreign to newcomers. In the outport of François, the authors found the music of the language to be pure West Country, a clue to British origins in the 17th and 18th centuries; their stories capture much of the the islanders' speech with its peculiar modulation of vowels and words with their endings unceremoniously dropped.

George Story, professor of English at St. John's Memorial University and a co-author of the *Dictionary of Newfoundland English*, points out that Newfoundland is a relic area, where idioms are preserved in local speech years after they have died out elsewhere. "There is an enormous creation of new words for new experiences and new weather," he explains, "for different plants, birds and fish and for the different technology of catching them. It's a matter of preservation and innovation without the constricting influence of a middle class, a class which did not exist in Newfoundland until recent times."

It seems ironic that a nomadic couple would be so smitten by a land which holds such strong ties on its inhabitants. Yva, who grew up in postwar Poland and emigrated to New York in the 1960s to work as an architect, and John, a New Zealander who left university mathematics for photography, have wandered the globe for most of their adult lives. Married in 1975 after a chance meeting on a back road in Wyoming, the pair has travelled throughout the world together, writing and photographing for such periodicals as *National Geographic* and *Equinox*. They established a home overlooking the Hudson Valley in upstate New York in readiness for the birth of their daughter, Tara, but along with her, still spend much of their life on the road.

As we sorted through a portfolio of photographs and transcripts of interviews gathered over seven years—the foundation of *This Marvellous Terrible Place*—Yva and John's obsession with the easternmost province of Canada became clear. Using the rugged landscape as a backdrop, they have captured the images and the voices that make both Newfoundland and Labrador so compelling. "The people spoke of hardship and hope, of daily bread and blood kin, of prejudices and tolerance, of resignation and defiance," Yva told us. Eloquent in the simplicity of their words, Newfoundlanders tell the story of their province, their land and their lives in a way that no sociologist or historian could ever hope to capture. Some speak with a knowledge of the outside world, while others offer the native insight and pride that come from the centuries-old traditions of outport life.

Conceived at first as a celebration of a special place, *This Marvellous Terrible Place* has become a stirring record of a way of life that has survived the rigours of 400 years—including four decades of Confederation.

Frank B. Edwards, associate publisher, September 1988

Puffins, Gannet Clusters

Yesterday we found a skipper, but the sea was too rough. Today we found a plane but no fuel. We are in the town of Cartwright in southern Labrador, trying to join scientists from the Canadian Wildlife Service who are studying Labrador's largest seabird colony on the Gannet Clusters. We talk to the crews on passing boats and hang around the wharf but have no luck at all. When you are stuck in Labrador, you have to let go of schedules and roll with events.

Cartwright is a haphazard gathering of clapboard and aluminum-clad houses and service buildings. Only some 650 people live here, but that is plenty for Labrador, where most settlements are even smaller and are often connected only by a seasonal ferry service or a winter highway of snow and ice, marked on maps as "snowmobile road with emergency shelters."

When French explorer Jacques Cartier anchored not far from here in 1534, he wrote, "In all the North Land, I did not see a cartload of good earth, yet went I ashore in the many places, and in the Island of Blanc Sablon, there is nothing else but mosse and small thornes scattered here and there, whitered and dry. To be short, I beleeve that this was the land that God allotted to Caine." Despite Cartier's indictment, European whalers, fishermen and explorers followed him to these barren shores.

Today, more than four centuries after Cartier's voyage, 32,000 people live in Labrador's 31 communities. There are about 1,200 Inuit, or Eskimos, on the north coast, some 800 Innu (Naskapi and Montagnais Indians) in the central part, 10,000 Settlers—the progeny of Inuit and Indian unions with European fishermen, whalers and adventurers—scattered among all the Labrador settlements and about 20,000 recently arrived outsiders. The entire population of Labrador would only fill a small Ontario town, and in a region larger than Newfoundland and the Maritimes combined, it all but disappears.

One day, we hear a helicopter. It lands by the wharf, and we run to make our pitch. Twenty minutes later, we are strapping our 2-year-old daughter, Tara, in her seat as the pilot pulls the throttle. Suddenly free, we spin into the sun and climb above Sandwich Bay, heading east toward the north Atlantic. Below us, Labrador lies resplendent, buckling as if from inner heat and sparkling with watery bloodlines of lakes, ponds and streams.

Where to? No landing is allowed on the bird islands; the breeding ledges are so smooth and sloping that the frantic movement of disturbed birds could dislodge their eggs. We land, instead, on a small deserted island a good distance from the study site, where we plan to wait for the scientists to pick us up in their boat. The pilot is concerned.

"I just can't leave you here," he argues, his face reddening with emotion. "No people, no shelter—and you with a small kid? No way. There is nothing here, nothing," he shouts above the whir of the spinning blades. But we stay, and he goes.

As the helicopter rears upward, we look around. Just below us, in a sheltered cove, a welcoming committee of seals breaks the surface and bobs in the water, necks stretching high, round eyes watching us with great curiosity. We move closer, and an eider duck catapults from its nest, leaving behind brown-spotted eggs and the softest feather imaginable. Lifted into the breeze, it flutters, alive, between our fingers. Out at sea, two huge castles of ice float by on their 1,000-mile trek south, their passage heralded by a flock of screaming seabirds. We know there are fish swimming underneath, feeding on the plankton plastered to the frigid hull. Between the icebergs, the black and white tail flukes of a humpback rise suddenly and then descend below the surface of the water in a slow-motion gesture of farewell. Is there really nothing here?

Late the next afternoon, the scientists' boat arrives and we leave. The sea rears in 10-foot swells, and we swaddle Tara in two life jackets to shield her against cold whips of spray. Suddenly, a wing-flapping armada of small stout birds with gaudy beaks zooms past. Puffins!

Our fear vanishes. Thirty-three thousand pairs of puffins, locally known as sea-parrots or hatchet-faces, nest on the Gannet Clusters, and hundreds surround us now. Notoriously poor fliers, they are superb underwater swimmers, darting below the surface in pursuit of capelin, their primary prey. Seabirds like these not only harvest their food from the sea but also, with their nitrate- and phosphate-rich wastes, fertilize the phytoplankton, microscopic plants that nourish tiny organisms called zooplankton. These are food for the fish, which are, in turn, eaten by seals, whales and seabirds, completing the cycle. Fishermen dislike the seabirds because they exploit the same niche of the sea, but they use them as unerring guides to the best fishing areas.

A small cove welcomes our boat, though our landing sends thousands of birds up in the air. We pitch our tent and go bird-watching, crawling carefully over grass made thick and healthy by tons of bird excrement and fish remnants. Puffin nesting burrows riddle the slope, but the parents are not home; they sit high above on the cliff's edge, rapping their huge bills together and ruffling the plump cheeks of their mates. Their guttural cry of *ha-aa ha-aa* fills the air. Farther down the shore, the ledges are crowded with birds standing shoulder to shoulder into the wind: elegant razorbills, looking like undertakers in black with white piping; fulmars, or noddies; black-legged kittiwakes, oddly nicknamed tickle-asses; and murres, known locally as turrs and much hunted for food. Despite the islands' name, there are no gannets: the cluster of rocky outcrops was named in the late 1800s not for its indigenous birds but for a British survey ship.

The night is as restless as the one on the deserted island: we are sharing our bedroom with 200,000 birds and dream winged dreams that explode at the first hint of dawn into a rattling, hysterical clamour of voices. Each spring, over three million seabirds return to a dozen island colonies around Newfoundland and Labrador just like this one. They are long-lived fowl—murres can live to be 30 years old, and gannets often reach age 50—but for every 100 chicks born, only five survive long enough to breed. Therefore, these birds nest close to reliable and plentiful sources of food, protected from predators by the steepness and remoteness of their breeding fortress.

Yet even here, on this precipitous granite slab in the midst of the watery desert of the north Atlantic, the birds are not safe. For hundreds of years, seabirds here have been hunted for meat, oil, fish bait and fertilizer, their nests robbed of eggs and their breeding grounds disturbed. It is little consolation that the eggs and meat were sometimes taken by men who had nothing else to eat, let alone to sell. Seabirds are also the unintended victims of heavy ocean traffic: they are caught in fishermen's gill nets and poisoned by ships' cargoes. Waterborne toxic chemicals, ingested from polluted fish, make the birds' eggshells thin and fragile, threatening the rate of reproduction. Each year, oil spills kill as many as 500,000 seabirds around Newfoundland, more than anywhere else in the American northeast.

The great auk is already extinct. Of the millions that once nested on Funk Island northeast of Newfoundland, all that remain are a pile of old skins, a scattering of bleached bones and one preserved specimen in a Copenhagen museum. On the Gannet Clusters, we overhear a marine biologist lament, "Sometimes I think we study them only so we'll know what we lost." We listen to the birds roar and think sombre thoughts.

August 1983

We are holing up in Nain, a village strung thinly along the shore of a small bay in northern Labrador. Two boys have moved into their parents' bed, and our family of three now occupies their concave cot. We are lucky to have that much, for lodging is hard to find in Nain.

Bill Ritchie, an artist who spends most of the year roaming with the Labrador Inuit and recreating their myths in his lithographs, said to us: "Go to the Terriaks. There are John, Johanna and their sons, Charlie and Titus. A fine family—they will treat you like they do everyone else." And that is how we came to live with an Inuit family in Nain, Labrador's northernmost settlement, with a population of about 900 people, most of them Inuit.

Once there were other settlements north and south of Nain, with biblical names like Hebron, Zoar and Ramah that echo 200 years of missionary presence. In 1771, members of the Moravian church settled in northern Labrador and began to exert spiritual, social and economic control over the Inuit. After World War I decimated the cod fishery and fur industry, the missions began to close and many Inuit left. Later, the Newfoundland government resettled the rest.

Tony Williamson, former director of the Labrador Institute of Northern Studies, told us about his 1956 visit to Hebron, one of the last remaining missions. The Inuit still lived in tents and sod houses, fished from skin kayaks and from trap boats fitted with a single-cylinder make-or-break engine. A pungent smell of decaying seal meat hung in the air. By contrast, the Moravian mission building, shipped from Germany in 1930, had great tile stoves, huge wooden beams, gleaming floors cleaned with sand, stuffed chairs and a good library.

The Inuit were being resettled that summer, and the missionaries were moving too. Tony remembers how Joshua Obed, the chief elder of Hebron, stood up and gave a speech. ''This is our home, and we don't want to leave,'' he said with tears rolling down his cheeks. ''But if we must, I'll lead the way for others.'' While the Inuit brass band stood among the rocks playing ''God Be With You Till We Meet Again,'' the Obed family piled into a trap boat and headed out of the bay toward Nain, one of the few mission settlements that survived.

Now, years later, there are problems in Nain. The growth rate in Labrador is about 4 percent per year, as high as in any Third World country, and since the creation of modern sedentary communities, the natural resources simply cannot support everybody. The rules established by Inuit elders, calling for orderly conduct in the community and on the hunting grounds, have been replaced by seldom-understood regulations, written in legal jargon and enforced by young RCMP officers. The young Inuit live in a particularly stressful no-man's-land. They no longer relate to the old ways, and even if they try they often lack the necessary skills. Yet they are ill-prepared to fit into white ways. In Nain, only five percent of Inuit children finish grade 10; those who drop out do nothing or try to find casual work at the fish-processing plant or with government programmes, but there are few jobs. Others start families and crowd the cottages of their relatives, getting on each other's nerves until they hit the bottle, each other or their kids. We see that for some people all purpose is gone, and they are perplexed, lost. Dependent on welfare, they lose their sense of control over their own destiny. Their alertness diminishes, and without it, they become too vulnerable for Labrador. There are accidents; there is suicide.

The weather here is terrible. It is August, and it snows. Nain is only as far north as Fort McMurray or Dundee, yet frigid air

John, Yva and the family dog Miś

John and Johanna Terriak on Dog Island

masses rush in from the icy waters of the Labrador Sea. It starts to blow, swirling around the water in the potholes along the main street and banging the loose windowpanes and crooked doors of the Inuit cottages.

Weather-bound, we stay home and cook with Johanna, read to the children and scrub them one by one in a large tin pan in the middle of the kitchen floor, using the same water because each cupful has to be lugged from a spring. We fight drafts in our room by pushing bits of newspaper behind the window frame. In a reassuring morning ritual, John Terriak hauls out the family's ''honey bucket,'' empties it into a nearby ditch, tunes the radio to the CBC news and settles down by his workbench, shaping dark pellets of silver into bright whale rings and miniature ulu knives that he and Johanna sell to newly arrived teachers and the nurses at the cottage hospital. It isn't much, but it keeps them off welfare. The Terriaks moved here from Goose Bay not long ago. They wanted to return to their Inuit roots, their families and the land; John is learning how to hunt and how to run his sled and the boat—how to be an Inuk, a man.

One morning, the sky is suddenly blue and the sea a huge pan of silver. John must feed his dogs, cloistered since early summer on a small island several miles south of Nain. The air is so translucent and calm that we all want to go. Our small wooden boat chugs slowly between the coastal bluffs, and in an hour, we see the rosy whaleback of the island, then the dogs bounding to a landing shelf on the sheer rock. Although John has not been able to get out to feed them for almost a week, they are fat and glossy: the island is ripe with berries, and there is water.

We feed the dogs and walk around. Before we know it, the wind picks up. John studies the mounting waves and says that we cannot go back to Nain. The sky is suddenly dark, clouds race, and we have no tent, no sleeping bags and no food. What we do have are three children. Charlie is 12 and quite strong; our Tara, though only 4, is robust and bundled in a snowsuit; but Titus, the Terriaks' younger boy, was born unwell, ravaged by a hereditary condition that makes his liver and heart huge but ineffective and his life a tentative proposition. We don't have his daily medication with us, and he is wearing only sneakers, blue jeans, a T-shirt and a thin windbreaker.

The men find an old wooden pallet and rebuild it with an axe, forming a small roof that they wedge into a thicket of black spruce, the only cluster of dwarfed trees on the stark face of the island. It starts to drizzle. The women cut branches, laying the fresh ones on the ground for bedding and breaking up the driest twigs to stoke the fire. As we gather the children between us, the huskies silently plop their wet bodies around the fire, their thick coats steaming. John takes his wife's small hands into his, bends down and blows warmly into the cool nest of her palms. She looks at him silently.

Night and worry come together. We keep the fire going, taking turns and talking in low whispers, and suddenly we see that this scene is a repetition of something that has happened thousands of times before—a small group of people huddling around a smoky fire on a stormy Labrador night. The morning comes grey and windy. We are concerned about Titus and tell the Terriaks that they should try to return without us, since each extra body means less precious freeboard in John's small boat. They hesitate but finally push off, and soon we cannot see them at all behind the frosty whitecaps. Did they go down? We worry, but we can only work at improving our shelter, walk briskly to warm up and wait. If they make it, we will soon hear the roar of the *Boston Whaler*, the RCMP boat, coming from Nain to rescue us. But the afternoon passes in silence.

Finally, there is a sound: an old-time trap boat heads straight toward the island, then veers off and heads westward, away from us. We yell and jump, trying to become 20 feet tall until—O glory be!—the boat turns back. We clamber aboard. The two Inuit have no idea who we are; they picked us up because of our frantic display on the rocks. The Terriaks? They didn't see them on their way from Nain, and nobody else has left the harbour all day— too windy.

We feel lucky but very worried. John had told us how inexperienced he was, and now his candour does not let us stop thinking about him, Johanna and the kids. The Inuit go to gather firewood in another bay, and it is evening before we return to the village and climb the familiar sandy road to the Terriaks'.

Charlie Terriak and sled dog

Johanna is in the window, her face soft with tears of worry. She says all of us would never have made it: their boat was taking water all the way to the nearest headland, so instead of heading for Nain, they left the boat there and carried Titus home, a long slog across the barrens. In Nain, they alerted the RCMP, but the police boat broke down, and Johanna was certain we would have to spend another night on the island.

In the evening, John Terriak comes to our room and says, "Somebody else could have taken that boat back with all of us. I couldn't, not yet." Then he adds simply, "But soon." And seeing how stubbornly he tries to find that missing link to his Inuit past, the sure footprints left by his ancestors on this land, we know he will. The room grows dark. We sit together by Titus, asleep and quiet under many covers, and for some reason, we ask John what "Terriak" means in Inuktitut.

"It means 'a weasel,' " he says. And he laughs.

December 1985

The coastal steamer enters the harbour, and the sickening roll of the cabin floor subsides.

We push open the metal door leading to the deck and step out. December night freezes on our faces. After 10 hours of rough sailing from Burgeo, we are docking in François (pronounced "Fransway"), a tiny outport on the wild sou'west coast of Newfoundland. The boat's spotlight licks the black surface of the sea, then picks out the dark timbers of the small government wharf. The light shifts again and suddenly finds people standing shoulder to shoulder, bulky in their winter clothes, shouting and waving while the steamer docks. As we tumble off the boat, released by the sea, the crowd greets its homecoming relatives and friends, kissing sleepy-eyed children and saying, "I can't believe how she's grown, boy" and "Did you bring Jack, too, dear?" Suitcases bulging with presents and bottles of rum are gathered up. It is midnight, but the windows are alight; the last steamer before Christmas has arrived.

Newfoundland joined Canada in 1949 after a bitter and much-contested referendum. When Joey Smallwood became the first premier of Canada's youngest province, he rushed to implement his vision of industrialization. Eager to bring cheap rural labour to industrial and mining towns, the new government moved to eliminate many of the existing 1,300 outports. Merchants stopped collecting the daily catch, schools were closed, and the mail service was suspended. But many outport families were in no hurry to join Smallwood's dream. The promised roads, electric power and steady jobs sounded just fine to people wresting their uncertain livelihood from the sea, but the prospect of relocating and abandoning what they knew best was disheartening and frightening. Bewildered, they saw their neighbours—the women in tears and the men locked in silence—packing and moving to "growth centres," anonymous townships away from home, where the promised jobs could not replace the sense of belonging they had left behind. One by one, the outports started to close down, like empty coffins.

It almost happened to François, and 20 years later, they still talk about it. Anxious and heartsick, the people here weathered out the bad times, while those from other sou'west coast communities—Parsons Harbour, Mosquito, Deer Island, Lock's Cove, Rencontre, Muddy Hole, Cul de Sac, Cape la Hune, Dark Cove and Fox Island—left their homes to snowdrifts and decay.

We settle in Gladys and Stuart Marsden's spare room behind the kitchen, with a quilt-covered bed and a neat stack of Bibles on a hand-embroidered towel. This is the first of the 12 traditional days of Christmas, and soon people will eat, visit and dance. Later, they will go mummering: disguised by masks, old clothes and bulky padding, they will bound from house to house with other unrecognizable creatures, something they no longer do in many other communities in Newfoundland. But for all this gaiety, we can see that people make do with very little.

Wedged between the barrens and the sea, between the winter ice and summer fog, the bright cluster of François houses occupies a narrow strip of land at the head of a deep fiord, just outside the shooting range of avalanches that tumble from the cliffs. The house paint peels readily after a year of storms, and the sea beyond the narrows roars with north Atlantic gales. Neither road nor rail links the village with the outside world. The coastal boat comes two or three times a week, weather permitting, which means it often does not come at all. Three local stores

François

Snowstorm, François

supply credit, a limited selection of predictable foods and ''François, Newfoundland'' T-shirts in basic colours. Entertainment means a game on the dimly lit pool table in Frank's store.

We count the fishing boats moored in the harbour, but there are not enough for all the families. When we ask Gladys what people do in François, she wrinkles her brow to remember and tells us that besides 28 fishermen, there are 8 lighthouse keepers, 5 store clerks, 3 storekeepers, 1 casual worker, 1 postmaster, 1 postal clerk, 1 water-system operator, 5 teachers (2 are not from François), 1 wharfinger, 2 powerhouse operators, 1 bait-depot officer, 1 electricity meter maid, 51 schoolchildren, 20 old-age pensioners and 2 people who run ''Greene's Take-Out.'' There are also the women who take care of their families and 21 young people, ''too old for school,'' who try to do ''things.'' What things? Well, baby-sitting, carpentry, storekeeping, even seasonal jobs on tugs in Halifax, she says. You must try anything.

This year, the role of ''Santa for Old Folks'' goes to Lloyd Greene, who has returned from Halifax to spend Christmas with his mother, Annie. Dressed in a red suit, he visits the old and infirm, delivering the gifts of canned Del Monte Pineapple Chunks in Heavy Syrup bought by the community. He has a ''drop'' with the men and invites the women, who remember him as a small boy, to sit on his lap. They snuggle up to him, their old faces suddenly backlit with a happy blush.

We share a drop with Lloyd.

''I left François at 17,'' he says. ''Halifax was scary—all these big buildings. And buses. I had no idea where they were going, so I used to walk everywhere. I worked for the Coast Guard, then on the offshore oil rigs. It's good pay.''

''Are François men envious of your life?''

''Not at all. They marry young, start families, have their lives all mapped out. They are so confident. They don't worry. Even if they get less education, they learn through living how to make what's needed and how to get along with each other. If I could get a job that would allow me to settle here, I would be happy.''

''Not too slow for you?''

''No. I've been in the fast lane long enough. Not much fun anymore. I would like it slow and sure and nice.''

The Durnfords, François

Behind Lloyd, the television screen brightens suddenly with the weekly instalment of "Land and Sea," a CBC documentary programme watched throughout the province with much reverence, perhaps because so many Newfoundlanders and Labradorians have starred in one of its segments or perhaps because they sense that its producer and director, David Quinton, admires them deeply.

"I'm constantly astounded at the ability of outport Newfoundlanders to make a living from the sea," Quinton told us once. "Some of them have been seafaring men who have travelled all over the world in command of vessels, and some of them, without a word of education, have lived quiet lives at home. Yet they have all done remarkable things. They live happily in what for many other people would be an inhospitable place. They can build a house and tell a story, make a fence and sing a good song or take an axe, go to the woods, find the right curve on a juniper stick and make the part of the boat they need, without any training or a blueprint. In their hands, this place becomes livable, and the axe becomes a tool instead of a weapon."

June 1987

The wind is sweet and warm, clinging to yellow flowers in small gardens and drying wings of flapping laundry behind houses. Just beyond the village of St. Vincent's, the road descends to the sea and sand pours over the edge of the blacktop.

A man bends over a dark ribbon parallel to the tidemark, which looks from a distance like a trail of sea litter. He picks something up and puts it into his bucket, moving slowly along the beach. We walk up to the ribbon. Capelin. Millions of smelt-like fish lie tossed upon the wet sand for as far as we can see, their lithe fish bodies already drying, their round eyes filmy and still.

Each June, capelin come to the beaches and coves of Newfoundland in untold numbers. Moving with an inner sense of purpose, the fish swim up in big schools, their midnight-blue backs darting in the foaming surf. Then when the time comes, they leave the only element that can sustain them and, drawn by an instinct as old as creation, fling themselves onto the sand to spawn in the snippet of time before another wave hits the beach. Their eggs, buried in the wet gravel by the sea, are soft underfoot

and safe from predators, but the spawning fish die.

Farther down the beach, Tara finds some live capelin. She carefully carries them to the sea where they belong, then watches sadly as they float listlessly, refusing to bolt back into the deep green. But this is how it is. This June in Newfoundland, the unending life chain unfolds daily before her, explaining itself. She watches the dance of salmon, the sudden breach of a humpback and the steep dive of gannets, all gorging on the seemingly inexhaustible capelin. She likes to munch on it too, when it is smoked and salty, and gradually learns about its role as the main food source for fish, marine mammals, seabirds and, indirectly, people.

The massive harvest of capelin by offshore foreign vessels in the early 1970s disturbed both marine scientists and Newfoundland fishermen. Since Canada introduced the 200-mile fishing zone, the stock has begun to recover. But inshore fishermen worry about draggers, which are guided by sophisticated instruments for detecting fish and are sweeping the sea clean with their huge nets. Fishermen talk about whales damaging their nets. Others are concerned about the enormous growth of seal herds, competing with humans for the cod stock, and the recent European ban on seal products, which all but terminated the annual seal hunt in Newfoundland. They mention parasites, carried by seals and passed on to cod. They all fear that soon the small inshore fisherman will go the way of the small farmer, and if that happens, the cherished social fabric of their lives will disintegrate.

The man we saw on the beach walks over to Tara and shows her his bucket full of capelin, trying to cheer her up. He says they are good for potatoes and she looks up at him, not comprehending. His name is Lawrence Gibbons, and he has been fishing most of his life, but now he is getting old and he likes the beach and his garden best. He invites us to his house.

Set off from the road beside a thicket of black spruce, the house shows infinite care; even truck-tire planters near the entrance are scalloped around the edges and finished with generous layers of red paint. Lawrence shows us a small dory he is building in the basement. The boat is already too big to make it through the door, and he will have to move the front wall to get it out when it is finished. On the way out, he touches the boat's clean, smooth ribs as if making sure that they still curve the way he wants.

The old garden outside is large, meant for feeding people who often get tired, hungry and cold. Not that Lawrence ever had much time to work on it; like many outport Newfoundlanders, he often has to leave home to feed his family. In the old days, it was the spawning of the humans that was a blessing and a curse.

Lawrence likes to put you in his shoes as he talks; this way, he knows, you may understand better.

"First, you have babies, and then you goes out to work; then you comes back and have more babies. Then you goes out to work for the railroad for nine months, and when you comes back home, your own children get right scared of you. They don't even know you. Oy, that's hard."

But he brightens up quickly, for it was a long time ago, and it is no use mulling over a pain half forgotten. After all, the sun is warm on his shoulders, there are visitors he doesn't mind talking to, and there is always more work to be done. He takes his bucket, walks to the potato patch and feeds the tiny fish to the soil, dropping the capelin, one by one, into the long, deep furrow.

Lawrence Gibbons, St.Vincent's

"Jack" and Lloyd Rideout, Cottle's Island

We were called barbarians. We were called crazy. We wanted the privilege to kill, beat the brains out of those young seals. We probably didn't even need the money—that's what the world thought we were like. But nobody kills seals because he likes to kill them.

We had an orphaned seal pup here one year. The mother probably got shot or caught in a net. An orphaned seal grows up to be a dwarf, what we call a "nog-head." Its head grows, but its body gets thin and long. It starves to death, bawling for its mother. A "screecher," some calls it. That's what this one was. It had wandered over the bay ice, probably 20 miles.

The bus driver saw him first, out on the ice. I knew he was going to be shot if he stayed out there, so I got the dory, went out and picked him up. He was wild, biting at me—drew blood. I brought him home in the pan of my pickup and carried him in my arms to the ice by my wharf. It was all froze over, but he got down in a crack in the ice. There was nowhere for him to go; he had to drown. I searched every crack. I figured he was too afraid and had gone under the ice and drowned.

I went out on the ski-doo late in the evening. I thought there might be a hole out there that he'd got into. I caught a glimpse of something black. When he saw me, he drawed down. I came back into the kitchen and said, "He's still there—I've just seen him. He's not dead. He's safe enough." I went out again, and he was up on the ice. I caught him in my arms. He was young and could get lost easily, so I carried him behind the wharf and put logs around, but it wasn't very long before he was over the logs.

I started to feed him canned milk. My daughter Nancy tipped some warm milk in a saucer, and we tried to get him to drink it. He'd just bite at the dish and almost break it. And he'd bawl. Every time he bawled, I threw some milk in his mouth. He was all in a mess, smeared with milk. The next day, I put out a net for herring. I would cut the herring open and get the milk out and put it on the ice for him. He was getting a bit quieter and licked at it. Then I gave him the roe, and before long, he would take strips of herring.

In a couple of days, he knowed me. When I went over the hill, he'd be out on the harbour somewhere, and he'd come whooping over the ice, waiting for the herring. He used to eat till he could eat no more. I don't think there was any end to him. He would eat his weight every day.

I never had my breakfast before he had his. I would see him within five minutes of getting out of bed. That seal got to me more than any dog I've ever had. I called him Jack.

During the day, I was getting my bait for my lobster traps and salting it down, and he was always right there. Everybody wanted to see him eat and would bring down herring and throw it out in the water and watch him come up from underneath. He had a lot of visitors, hundreds. I put a bit of white paint on his nose and red ribbon around his neck so he wouldn't get shot.

Once he swam out and got in a net. I jumped in a speedboat, and when I got there, the bobbers on the net were going crazy. I got him free, but he slipped away. I had a nice piece of herring, and when he came up, I grabbed him under the chin. He tried to scratch me with his flipper, so I grabbed it and hoisted him in the boat. He did some fighting; he wanted to get out some bad. I had to hold him between my legs. I said, "I've just done something that was never done before." When I landed the boat, I took him in my arms and put him on the front seat in the pickup. He upped to the window with his nose, trying to get out. By the time I got in on the driver's side, he was there, biting at me.

When the ice all thawed out, he wanted to leave and go on. But it was the start of lobster season, and there were lots of herring nets everywhere. He'd only get tangled up in one and shot, so I built a pen to put him in, and he did not like that at all. He got out one night. It was dark, and I couldn't find him. The next morning, I got up at 4 o'clock. I attached a big piece of gill net to the paddle and the gaff. I was going to shuffle the net under the water and feed him to get him to swim over the net. I'd quickly pinch the ends together and roll him in the boat. If only I had seen him, I knows I'd have gotten him. But I searched all day and never saw him.

Lloyd Rideout, sealer/fisherman, Cottle's Island

Parsons Harbour

Hove away

When we left the wharf, it was thick with fog there. I said to myself in my mind, I don't want to see it. And in the fog and stuff, I didn't.

Leaving behind your home that you built with your own hands and your fishing gear that you'd worked with all your life—left behind, gone. You were coming to another place, and you weren't going back no more. All the years gone by, simply hove away.

Theodore Symes, formerly of Parsons Harbour

We was forced out

It was leaving behind a way of life you were brought up to. It was different, definitely different. If we went into the country and killed meat, we'd share with everybody. We'd cut up the meat, wrap it up in paper, carry it to the other houses and pass it in. What one had, we all had.

First one family went, then another, and once it got down to a pretty small crowd, the young ones wouldn't stay there. I don't know if you'd call it we was forced out, but that's what I would call it.

It was hard packing up to leave. We sold our dory and all our fishing gear. Gave it away for next to nothing. We rolled the crockery in clothes and put it in old pork barrels. We crated the oil stove and took it down to the wharf with a handbar. Put the mattresses in plastic.

We took the cat. She travelled in a cardboard box that we put holes in. We had the two children, 5 and 3 then.

The hardest thing ever I done was when I gave up my dog. I gave it to a fella from Grey River. He tied on the wharf, and I led the dog over. Juno was his name. He was old then. We used to use him for country work in the woods in the wintertime. We'd hunt caribou. We weren't supposed to, but everybody used to. We'd take our dogs, harness them up, and they'd help haul the caribou out.

We went to Burgeo first. I worked in the fish plant a year. Then we had to do it all over to come up here to Port aux Basques.

I never want to do it again.

Ivan James, formerly of Parsons Harbour

in your fingers. I could look down and see the bone. In the morning, they were right stiff. And pups—boils from your elbows down, from your jacket rubbing the wet skin. You talk about sore. Oh, blessed Virgin who's dead. Oh, misery.

Three thousand pounds for a dory, and maybe you would jig three boatloads for a day. They were big fish then. They could eat the ones fishermen catch now. For lunch.

All the big fish are caught. Only the young are left, and them are getting scarce. Too many fishermen for too few fish, and the whole world is out there catching them.

Lawrence Gibbons, retired fisherman, St. Vincent's

Fisherman, Nippers Harbour

Jigging

Oh, I loves the sea. I loves the sea. I understands the sea a lot. Now there is people afraid of the sea. I don't know why; they must have a reason. But me, I loves the sea.

Now you've got to respect the sea; you have to learn how to work together. You have to work to live. If you don't feed yourself, someone else has to do it. I did fish trapping, and I did fish trawling. Oh yeah, and jigging. Jigging with a piece of lead—that's for the birds. That's OK if you are on holiday, but to go and make your living with a jigger and the line cutting into the bone in your hand?

My dad and me would jig fish in shoal water. A steel hook, stuck into a big fish. Twenty pounds of wild fish, just five fathoms down. You haul in 150 of them, your hands wet and line slipping on your fingers. By and by, the skin comes off, and then the salt water eats away your flesh, right into the bone. Big holes

Jigging cod, Sally's Cove, Gros Morne National Park

Arctic foxes

Time was boring. I was working with Bell Telephone in the eastern Arctic. There were Arctic foxes around. I used to take a 44-gallon oil drum, cut the head out and make a pivoting top with a piece of metal pipe, a bit like a rubbish can. I'd dig the barrel down in the sand on the beach, just above the high-water mark, and put bait down into it. The foxes would smell the bait, step on the cover and down they'd go, into the barrel.

I'd put on a big pair of welder's gloves, an Arctic parka. Then I'd get my hands down and take one up. I'd nip his four paws in one hand, and he'd snarl at me. His lips would come right up over his nose, and you'd see all his front teeth. I'd talk to him and smooth him down, stroking the back of his neck with my other hand. By and by, he'd gradually relax. Maybe I was the first human being that ever he saw. When I let him go, he'd make three or four quick runs, stop and look back at me for a second. Then he'd be gone.

Jack Troake, fisherman/sealer, Harts Cove

Western Brook Pond, Gros Morne National Park

Gros Morne National Park

Western Brook Pond

We were possibly the first women to take a canoe in there. A southeasterly gale whipped up, which is no mean thing—or a very mean thing. When the wind died down, we took to the water. The canoe was so tiny, and the cliffs so big, so sheer. We paddled close, brushing our hands against them: great rough and rugged pinnacles with broken edges. In places, we looked up from beneath their shadow into the light till we were dizzy.

It was the height of spring, and the leaves were just out. Who would have thought that in that vast place, a mile or so wide, it would be the roar of birds singing that stole our attention? Fairly close to us, a wren sang in full voice, his high-pitched, melodious song varying from beginning to end. I remember it as well as I remember the texture of the rock against my fingertips.

Pat McLeod, artisan/writer, Curzon Point

About halfways around the pond, we heard "bang! bang!" A moment later, "bang!" Next, we saw a moose swimming across the pond. Terry and Dave said, "They missed."

"No," I said. "They got one. I heard the finishing shot."

I was 13 then, and I had heard stories from my uncles about that finishing shot. It wasn't moose season, so we were not only suspicious but excited. We knew my neighbour Jack was around the pond with his son Woodrow and my cousin Derek.

When we reached their spot, Jack was fishing—all kinds of line out, really working hard trying to catch a fish.

"How's the fishing, Jack?"

"Nothing at all, boy. There are a couple of trout in there."

"Where's Derek?"

"Oh, he's up there, getting a bit of wood for the night."

"Where is Woodrow?"

"He's gone across the brook to see if there are any bakeapples."

Just the way he said it, we knew Woodrow was with the moose, so away we went, across the brook, with Jack hollering, "No need for any of you young fellows to go over there this evening." There was Woodrow, just paunching the moose, a yearling. Was he ever upset, caught red-handed. Then his father and Derek turned up, and the three of them were telling us to go back to our camp and not mention it to anyone. We had a little powwow of our own and decided we were getting in on the act.

"We'd like some of that meat," we demanded.

After a bit of discussion, Jack agreed; he knew we could get to the RCMP long before they could get the meat home and hid away. He decided he and Woodrow would have a quarter each; Terry, Derek, Dave and I, half a quarter each. We quickly quartered the moose with the skin still on, brought it back across the brook and, slipping and struggling, headed back 'round the pond.

When we reached camp, we tucked it away and cleaned ourselves up. We got the fire going and boiled the kettle. Everybody was beat, and the boys began to turn in. I noticed Jack wasn't moving. If the old bugger wasn't turning in, neither was I. I didn't trust him.

The fire was still going. Around midnight, he and I had another cup of tea and roasted some capelin. They were delicious and revived us somewhat. I was expecting that any minute, Jack would say this was enough and turn in. But, no, he stayed awake.

Around 2 o'clock, he reached into his pack and out came an orange. Oh my, how delicious that looked in the firelight, especially knowing how great it would taste after that salty capelin. He hauled out his knife and cut the orange into eight pieces without peeling it. Then he laid the pieces next to the fire and very unhurriedly and methodically ate each piece. He would slide his thumb between the peel and the orange, then suck slowly until he finally pulled off the peel and flicked it into the fire. In a matter of probably a half an hour, he ate the whole fruit.

My lips were drying up by the minute. I was becoming quite agitated. But you know, it was kind of good because it kept me awake. I wasn't slowing down at all, because I was mad. When he finished sucking the orange, he sat back and waited until dawn started to break. "Might as well get the other boys up," he said, and those were the first words that he had said since that orange appeared.

We skinned the moose quarters, cut them into more manageable pieces, packed them in our bags, then headed home. I got there about 20 after 7. Dad was just going to work. When he saw what was in my pack, he was surprised and glad, because we could use the meat. He wasn't unknown to have gotten meat out of season himself. I was proud and concerned he should see that I wasn't even tired. But as soon as he went to work, Mum said, "Go to bed now." And I didn't stir much until noon, by which time she had it all bottled up and my pack washed out. There wasn't a trace anywhere, except the bottles of meat bathed down and hidden away in the cupboard.

It comes to me sometimes when I sit quietly and peel an orange. That was an important episode in my adolescent life. Since that night, Jack's impression of me changed. I was no longer a wee child. I had stood my ground. We became hunting partners and buddies.

Gary Pittman, boat builder, Rocky Harbour

Brothers, Great Northern Peninsula

When we lived in Goose Bay, my father used to tell me a story about a little orphan boy who lived with cruel people. They were beating him up and feeding him scraps that fell in the dirt. One night in the summer, he went up on the hill and met a little bird. The bird made the boy strong, so he picked up big rocks and threw them on the houses of the people who had treated him bad. He killed them all.

Goose Bay wasn't my part of the country. White people there treated us as inferiors; they were always pointing at me, calling me "Skimo." But I went to trade school in St. John's when I was 18 and lost my inferiority complex. I became a hard fellow and wouldn't take anything anymore. I would argue. I learned I was just as good as anyone else.

Even here in Nain, people tell me to go back to Goose Bay because I'm not from here. But this talk has died down. I told them off, had a few fights. I don't worry about fitting in; I just want people to stop telling me I don't belong here. I'm not like

Terriak Family, Dog Island, Nain

John Terriak, Nain

everybody else. I'm a carver. They're either working or on unemployment or on welfare.

I sleep good in Nain. In Goose Bay, I was haunted by ghosts. I used to wake up in the night and my ear was ringing, the hair on the back of my neck was sticking up and I couldn't move. I was right scared. One night I woke up and white shadows were trying to get into bed with me. They were ghosts. After I came to Nain, it all stopped. I only felt one ghost the first week we moved in. I had a pan in my hand, and something pulled right hard on it. Later, Johanna held the same pan, and something pulled on it too.

We came here with two kids, $14 and no place to stay. All we had were the clothes on our backs—no blankets, nothing. When we arrived, everything was new and exciting. I learnt about the sea. I learnt about the land and how to make a snow house. I learnt about good ice and bad ice. I learnt how to travel in a blizzard. In a blizzard, the wind usually blows in one direction, and if you know the landmarks, you can use the wind to set your course. I asked lots of questions. People got tired of me asking questions. I'd watch others, then go off by myself. I don't plan ahead; I just do things.

Now, I get much of our food from the land. Our dogs eat richer than the welfare people. They have char, caribou, seal, codfish, partridge and duck. Even our cat is fussy about what she eats. She doesn't like cat food very much. She'd rather have trout and deer and seal.

John Terriak, artist/hunter, Nain

Poppy's valentine

My grandmother was a midwife and the wisest woman I ever met in my life: Sarah Ann Farwell. She was blind for 40 years. She had the first cataract operation performed in Newfoundland, but something happened and she got an infection in that eye. It spread to the other eye, and she lost them both. She was over 70 then. She learned Braille, got herself a pack of Braille playing cards, and she learned to type. You just could not stop her; she had so much faith.

She used to say, "Don't think about dying. All you do is pass on to another life. Don't worry about it. You get ready for your birthday—that is a great time. You get ready for death—that is a great time too."

Near the end of her life, she went into a coma for about a week. It was winter, a really stormy time. My mother and aunts were taking turns beside her. One day, she woke up and said, "Wouldn't I like to have a lovely strong cup of tea. It seems ages since I had some tea. It is really stormy outside, isn't it? I can hear the storm beating against the window. I bet anything people around this town are saying, 'This is Sarah Ann's storm; it is going to take her away.' " In those days, that was the thing. A really stormy day could bring a birth or a death.

"But I'm not going," she said. "Not at this time of the year. I never did want to die in winter, with frozen ground and giving everybody such a hard time digging a grave. I'm not going to die yet. Now if I have my way, and most likely I will, I'll die before the capelin spawn, before the men get busy with the capelin. When spring is here and the flowers are out. When everything is fine." She got up and had her tea. Sure enough, that year in June, she died before the capelin came.

I used to sit there, just rubbing her hands and getting her to tell me all the beautiful stories about the time when she was growing up. I would love to have lived in her era. She would tell me about Christmastime, how they would prepare for weeks ahead. They

Anglican Church, Fogo Island

34

would make presents. They would hide them, take them out when no one was around and work on them a little more. My grandfather would make cradles and wooden toys, and my grandmother had a fantastic way of making dolls. She would make cotton bodies and stuff them with wood shavings and paint their faces. She was great. If you were sick and went to her, you felt better just touching her.

My father had a sawmill and a two-storey mill house. I would stay up with him all night while he was making caskets. I used to think it was a lonely job, so I would go and sit and chat with him. He was the dearest, sweetest person. He would take shavings from the boards and slip them in my hair. I would have all these golden ringlets from the cover of a casket throughout my blonde hair. It is just the most beautiful thing to think of.

Mom and Dad died within two weeks of each other. It was sad at the time, but that was how they wanted it. They had a book. Everything they wanted us to do at the time of their deaths was written there—all the funeral arrangements, what clothes they wanted, who they wanted for bearers. They lived long enough to celebrate their golden anniversary. It was just like the nice

ending chapter of a lovely story. Looking back on it now, it was a happy occasion. Sad, but happy.

Dad died on the 25th of January, and just two weeks later, Mom died. She was buried on Valentine's Day. We went into the church the night before. My mother's body was lying there, and there was a basket of flowers in the church that had been sent to Dad's funeral two weeks earlier. My little niece noticed them. There was one carnation sticking up in that basket, just the same as if it were freshly picked. She went over and snipped it off and tucked it into the collar of my mother's dress. ''Here's a valentine that Poppy saved for you,'' she said.

It took away all the tension.

Lorna Stuckless, museum curator, Twillingate

Marvellous Funks

My most incredible experiences were always on Funk Island, because it is such a hard place. I go to the Funks with the Sturges from Valleyfield, good longline fishermen who have always fished there. Their phrase for the Funks is "this marvellously terrible place." And that's what it is, marvellously terrible.

The fishermen row you over in a dory, and you feel for them because they really risk their lives to put you on the Funks. Then you wait for a wave to jump on what we call "the bench," a foot-wide rock ledge in the cliff, that is slippery and narrow. A hard place to carry up supplies, but there are little man-made grooves in the rock to put your fingers in. The Beothuk Indians used to go there in the summer for great auk eggs, probably landing on the same shelf.

The Funks are legendary. This is a graveyard of the great auks, now extinct, and of the sealers who died there. There is a small grassy meadow, riddled with puffin burrows and old corrals, where people used to herd the great auks. They slaughtered the birds, which couldn't fly, picked the feathers, rendered the fat and oil and threw the birds away, so now there are piles of thousands and thousands of bones. And feathers—I bet you could still find an old great-auk feather mattress in some deserted house in Bonavista Bay.

Puffin, Witless Bay Sanctuary

Once on the island, you learn to cope. Your tent goes down in the middle of the night in a high wind. It's cold. You worry about hypothermia. You are alone, but you live through it. Outside, there are just birds—everywhere. You are overwhelmed; you've never seen so many, shoulder to shoulder. You've never seen so much life at one time. Once, I couldn't conceptualize a single bird anymore. It was like looking at ants. When you walk around, you know you've never seen so much death either. Smothered

Kittiwakes, Witless Bay Seabird Sanctuary

chicks, smashed eggs, piles of bones. On the Funks, life is visibly coupled with death and death with life.

After your work is all done, you return with one of the fishermen on his boat. Then you sit in his kitchen with his wife, and she makes you tea, so you always feel as if they are your parents. The fishermen are so clean, the way they live. And you jump into the best part of their lives, which is fishing, and then you jump out. You don't have to stay there during the hard or boring times. You just share their adventures.

Usually, you are emotionally charged when you come back, especially when you've been out among the birds for weeks and months. And you always feel like you want to cry. It probably happens when you come back from living close to whales or seals too—a strange, warm feeling. A real part of the job, although it has nothing to do with what we do, but it's incredibly important. It happens all the time.

William Montevecchi, ornithologist, St. John's

My children didn't know me

I was reared by a stranger. I went to sea when I was 15 years old. Skipper John Parson, that's who I went to sea with, and he was like a father to me.

One time, he arrived here in the schooner, anchored and came into the house. My mother told him, "John, Bill wants to go to St. John's, to see the city." I was only a boy then, and there was nothing around here. "Yes," he said. "Put a bit of clothes together for him, and tell him to come on if he wants to see St. John's." For somebody of my years to go to St. John's, it was a wonderful thing.

So I went just for a trip, that's all. That was in August month, 1936. I was a young devil for climbing, go up on the mast, anywhere at all. When we came to Indian Bay, the cook got sick and had to go home. Now they had no cook, and they wanted me to take it on. "Well, gee," I said. "I don't know how to boil the kettle." The skipper's brother said, "Come on, Moose, young bugger"—"Moose," he always used to call me—"I'll show you

how to put on the duffs and make the pudding." And I learnt.

I left school with grade three. Well, Skipper John was not hard to me, but he was right there on my back to see me learn. He would get down and show me how to tie that knot or strap that barrel. And the chart: whenever he would go to take off a course, he'd say, "Come here, Moose. I'll show you what I'm doing here." After a couple of years, I didn't want Skipper John or no one to tell me, because they had already taught me. Local knowledge—it was hard and sound. You didn't forget it.

Old town, St. John's

I was with them five years. After that, I went almost all over the world: West Indies, Greenland, Northwest Territories. Wherever I could see the most dollars, I went. I worked at it all, from skipper to engineer. I was chief cook with the railways. I worked in Churchill Falls as a diamond driller. I went to Ungava, operating a boat for Fenimore Iron Mines. I worked in a machine shop in Toronto, operating a forklift. I was deckhand on the lake boats under Ontario Power, and I skippered boats for different people.

My children, my wife reared. They didn't know me. My oldest daughter is in Toronto. She scarcely knew me for a father. I was never home, winter or summer. I would come home perhaps for a week or two and was gone again. That was the only way I could see to live. I thought if I didn't have the dollar for them to get their education, well, they were going to probably be like myself and have to try to get through life the hard way. I would have liked to have had the education, but if I was to go and get my deep- sea certificate, it would have taken 8 or 10 months, and I never had the money for my family to live on for that length of time.

I took a heart attack when I was 53. That was 12 years ago. Last spring, I had an operation in St. John's for my circulation. And I still won't give up. I'll still go if I can move. I always used to.

William Norman, retired cook/skipper, Newtown

John Marsden catnapping, François

Toronto

The best part of farming is the change. There is always change. One day, you are making hay. Before you get a chance to get tired of it, you are cutting turnip off the field. And before you get a chance to get tired of that, you are butchering beef. You are only at that a little while, and there is something else. It always changes. You never get bored with it.

We had visitors last week from Toronto. They are busy up there, trying to make a living—scrabbling. It reminds me of that big barn over there, across the river, with chickens in cages. The chicken gets fed in the morning; she lays her egg at 3 o'clock; she gets fed again at 7 o'clock; then she roosts. It is all routine. She knows what she's going to do and where she is going to be the next day, and them fellows are the same—every day, every day, every day, except for two weeks' holiday. It is an awful way to live, as far as I'm concerned.

Leonard Downey, farmer, Doyles

Me playing the fiddle

My grandmother had an old fiddle. It was hung on the wall for years. It had got a couple of holes broke into it, which I could have helped do as a kid. This Christmas Eve when I was 11, they were dancing in our house. This old fellow played the fiddle, and I listened to him most of the night. The next day, I told Mother I was taking the old fiddle home; I was going to learn to play. ''I doubt you'll learn on that,'' she said.

Father patched it up. He boiled some caribou skin and made glue, then put blue birch rind over the holes. It never came off. There were two strings on the old fiddle: one gut string—that was the third string—and the bass. He took a strand out of a lobster line and made the second string. In those days, we used a waxed thread for sewing skin boots. You couldn't break it; you had to cut it. That's what he used for my first string. It would do me a little while, then it would get right woolly, and there would be no sound to it, so I had have to cut myself another one. The bow had no hair on it; Father put sewing cotton one end to the other, back and forth, and made a bow. I had raw spruce gum I picked off the trees to rub on it.

Father could play a bit, so he put my fiddle in tune a few times and showed me the strings—how these fingers were high and those were low. I had no trouble to learn it. I picked it right up, just by the sound. Uncle John Peter Payne and Leonard Payne, they used to play all the dances till I got to 15. I started then, so the younger ones didn't have to trouble the older fellows. In Daniel's Harbour, we used to play a lot in Al House's big kitchen. It was 20 feet square, a stove over on one side. You'd clear out the chairs and put the table back in the corner, kerosene lamps on the table. Twenty-five or thirty people might come. They danced with their rubber boots on, and in the wintertime, everybody had sealskin boots. Right light on their feet, you'd hardly hear them. It was like a swish as they were swinging around, me playing the fiddle and the crowd dancing.

Rufus Guinchard, fiddler, Hawke's Bay

I was named after a great saint, Saint Joseph. He was a carpenter, but I didn't follow up on him that way. I'm a fisherman.

I've big marks on my arms from saltwater pups. They'd get all infected, and my hands would swell right up. I'd take my pocket knife and cut open my gloves to put them on. But you had to go; you had to do it.

We have six children—three boys and three girls. Liola and Joe, they learned to fish with me. I used to take their mother along because they wasn't afraid of me, but they was afraid of her. She fished with us for years, a strong woman. She'd stand behind the hydraulic winch, she'd pull the nets, and we'd clear out behind her. The three of us would take out the codfish, the flounder and the crabs. She'd keep the boat going ahead into the wind.

We'd bait our hooks in the nighttime. We'd go away before dawn. When we got the trawls all set, we'd make a good fire, boil the kettle, toast up some bread and a bit of fish and have our lunch. I'd always cook. My wife said I was a better hand for cooking fish than she was. It was probably an excuse, but I believed her. After lunch, we'd haul back our longlines. We'd get in about midday and sell our fish. We'd go out again in the evening, to jig squid for bait. They'd squirt this awful black dye into our eyes, and when we came home, it would take us half an hour to wash ourselves before we could go to bed.

It wasn't an easy job, but it was joyful. There was something about it. The sun came out of the water in the morning. You'd hear the birds singing and whistling, and if there was fish on your longline, you didn't care if the world hung upside down.

To be a doctor in Canada, you've got to go to college for six years. To be a good fisherman, a prosperous fisherman, you also have to go to school. You have to learn to mend and how to knit your nets, make sails and traps, repair or build your boat. You've got to be a carpenter. You've got to build your own house. You've got to be a meteorologist: know the weather, the moon and the stars, the tides and the winds and where the fish congregate at a certain time. When the water temperature changes, you must know whether to set your nets deeper or shallower.

I have more respect for a fisherman than I have for any doctor. To be a fisherman, you've also got to be a damn good man. You've got to be a family man. You've got children to rear. You've got to teach them too. You've got to be a teacher. Then, you had to be a cobbler. You had to sole your own shoes. You had to put heels on them. You went to the general store, and you bought pieces of leather and cobbler tacks. If you were going to go to a dance that night, you couldn't put too many tacks in your shoes—they'd make too much noise. The woman, she taught her daughter how to sew with the sewing machine. She showed her how to make an apron, how to make a dress. If they were to go to a dance, they made their own clothes.

The Grand Banks are being cleaned up. The big companies are sweeping up all the fish that's out there. All Europe is out there and all North America. Nothing can withstand that. It's a pity. The Portuguese came here and got hundreds of years' fishing out of her, but they fished with only one hook. Plenty of men, but one hook for each little dory. There'd be fish for the whole world if everybody fished like the Portuguese. But big business got into it, and greed got into it. We had to fatten up England. We had to fatten up France. We had to fatten up all Europe.

The biggest damage is being done on the famous Hamilton Banks. That's where the fish spawn in January and February. The big companies have put heavy steel bows on their trawlers and made them twice as big and twice as strong so they could go there and catch the fish right when they're beginning to spawn.

If you goes killing the hens when they are laying the eggs and you kill all the sheep when it comes time to lamb, you can't have no eggs, you can't have no lambs. Take all the young women away, and you won't have no children. And the business people know it twice as well as I know it. Cut down on the big companies, put every fisherman on a quota, put a moratorium on the Grand Banks, and by Jove, she'll come back. Twenty years' time, she'll come back, and half the loaf is better than no bread any time.

Joseph O'Brien Sr., retired fisherman, Bay Bulls

He fishes

Dad? He fishes, but he doesn't need his fish. If you smile, he's got his fish.

Joe O'Brien Jr., co-owner of Bird Island Charters, Bay Bulls

Fishermen empty a cod trap, Conche

Woman and rooster, St. Bride's

Please don't serve me barbarous

People spoke old English, very colourful. Once, a woman came in and wanted me to remove her lower molar. I thought perhaps I could fill it, save it for her. I was trying to educate people to have fillings done. She said she wanted her tooth "'auled," as in hauling a net. So I asked, "Does it pain?" And she said, "No." So I said, "Does it ache?" And she said, "It's not a *h'ache*, it's a *h'agony*." "All right," I said, "I will take it out." "Very good," she said. You see, a "h'agony" was a dreadful pain.

Another man asked me to make him a gold tooth. He travelled a lot and showed me a little gold inlay on one of his teeth. "This here attracts women," he said. "But if you make me a whole gold tooth, there would be no holding me back at all."

People were very descriptive. They were so afraid because they were treated badly by amateurs taking out teeth. They would say, "Please don't serve me barbarous." They also had superstitions. I had a patient, a fairly educated man, with a very bad molar I wanted to remove. But he said, "Oh, no. I have to keep 'e"— they referred to teeth as "he" or "she," with an "h" or "sh" dropped—"because 'e was charmed by a faith healer."

They went to any hardship to help others and would bring patients from a long way out. They would lash them down with ropes in their small open boats, travelling for many miles, protecting them. Or they might walk across ice fields and snow, hauling a sledge, making sure the sick one was comfortable. Then they had to wait often for days before they could go home

One day, a girl came in with her mother. She had only one cavity, but her mother wanted that tooth out. "No," I said, "it should be filled." The mother said, "Take it out. I can't have this child suffer all winter." While she was in the waiting room, I filled the tooth, and when she saw it, she was extremely cross with me. But next spring, she came and brought me a whole carton of Camels—very expensive, a big present. I said, "Why did you change your mind?" "Oh," she said, "the Mountie came to visit and told us you did the right thing."

Another problem arose while making dentures. You were trained at dental school to make teeth to suit the face: a strong man should have big, strong teeth, and a pretty little lady should have rounded or oval teeth. Teeth are the same shape as your face. But in Twillingate, everybody wanted the same size teeth. One day, I made dentures for a truly small woman, so I made her very tiny teeth. Then her husband came, and I made him beautiful masculine teeth with a good expression. Next spring, he had no teeth again. I asked, "Where are your teeth?" He said, "I threw them across the h'ice. They were hound's teeth, too big." Then he added, "I want the same you've made for me wife. They were nice. I'm paying for them. I'm getting me teeth as I want them."

Nowadays, everything is changed. There are roads, television. They don't speak the old English in Twillingate anymore. They speak American or Canadian. Or just Toronto.

Michael Maguire, dentist, St. John's

Young girl, Codroy Valley

again. They were good and kindly, with never any thought for themselves.

People were patient. They had taken a lot of abuse; they had put up with much suffering. Many would come to have all their teeth out, even though they were good, because they were afraid of a winter with pain. I can sympathize: once I had to remove my own wisdom tooth in the middle of the winter.

Mature harp seals on pack ice, Flat Rock

My ancestors were rogues and murderers and pirates

I think it was right and proper to stop killing the white-coats. I hunted them 11 years. There was nothing else we could do to make one penny at that time of the year. So Jesus, what could we do? I had a house full of kids. I had to feed them, clothe them, give them an education. If you can go and kill white-coats and make $400 or $500, what do you do? Not go and kill white-coats because someone in New York said that you can't go and kill them, that it's a crime? To me, that's bloody ridiculous. But times have changed, and we haven't got to do that anymore.

When a harp seal is born, it has a yellowish cast for about 48 hours, then it turns pure white; that's your white-coat. After two weeks, it turns a sooty colour. We call them "raggedy jackets" then. The old harp has got a coal-black saddle the shape of a harp on its smoky-grey back. It's beautiful, but seals are beautiful anyhow. They're much prettier than dogs. You can watch them through the telescope sight before you shoot. You see their nostrils opening and closing and their great big eyes—beautiful.

I've never seen any fun in killing yet. I love animals—any kind.

I can't recall ever killing an insect, but I can kill seals. I can take a gun in my hands right now and shoot a thousand seals and have no problem with it when I really need the money. But if I went out and killed a thousand seals and then jumped on a plane to Florida, blew the money and came back home, I'd say, "Don't kill another seal, you don't need it." I'd join the Greenpeace.

We've got an enormous seal herd. If we're to maintain a fishery, we must have a seal fishery. The people the protest movement is trying to convince must be awful stupid. We've been killing seals in this province for over 400 years. We can go on killing 180,000 a year for the next 1,000 years. That's how strong our seal herd is.

The politicians put the ban on sealskins, but the people still want to buy them. The United States issued the first ban, and other countries have followed suit. I can understand the United States; if they choose to ban seal products, that's their business. But we originated from Great Britain. This bloody little rock of ours was populated by our ancestors who came here because there were two things: fish and seals. When Britain went along with the States and put a ban on seal products, I said, "I'll never sing God Save the Queen, the King, Prince Charlie or any of them." My ancestors were rogues and murderers and pirates from Great Britain. We've been here for a long time. We're starting to get more civilized now. We're kindhearted people, but I hates like hell to be used and dictated to.

I'm an independent fisherman. I owe no man anything—not a cent. I'm uneducated, but I don't give a damn. Give me an old punt, a one-clawed jigger and a shotgun, and I'll always go to bed with a full belly. You can't say that for someone in Toronto.

We never had a big lot of money, but we always had enough to pay our bills, and we always had clean underwear put aside in the bedroom. When I got my hand all tangled up in the winch belt, that's the first thing that came to my mind. I came to the house with my hand wrapped up in a towel and told Florence to slacken my belt and strip me right down. That's all she took off me: my drawers. She put on the clean ones and hauled my pants on again. I went up to the hospital then.

Jack Troake, fisherman/sealer, Harts Cove

Jack Troake, Harts Cove

Sledding, François

Tricks

People overcame the isolation by playing tricks on one another. There was a man who used to boast a lot. Whatever he had or did, he thought it was better and bigger than anyone else's. So people said, ''We must bring him down a peg.''

Most people had a pig to fatten up for Christmas. They killed it in early December and let the meat mature in the cool weather. This man killed his pig too, and it was going to be the best pig ever. Somebody decided to teach him a lesson and hide his pig under the fish flake so he wouldn't have it for Christmas. People rubbed it in throughout the holidays, and when Christmas was over, the pig was returned. He suddenly discovered it in the shed and didn't know if he had gone crazy or not.

Canon George Earle, St. John's

Sarah Durnford, François

Wee drinks

I wish there were only three days in the year: Christmas Day, payday and Sunday.

Funny, but we thinks of Christmas all year, even in July. I might come in with my boat, and somebody wants a couple of fish. ''How much do I owes you, Eli?'' he asks, and I says, ''That's all right.'' So he says, ''I'll catch up with you at Christmas.''

At Christmas, he yells, ''I owes you a drink, old man. Come in, come in.'' And all those big fish turn into wee drinks.

Eli Skinner, fisherman, François

Whaling

Whales know when you're after them. Some of them come clean out of the water and take off so fast there's no way you can catch up with them. A whale travelling undisturbed has a certain pattern, so we used to time them. Three, four, five minutes and he'd blow again. Five minutes, then three minutes, then back to five. You'd adjust your boat speed gradually, because if you changed your sound in the water too rapidly, he'd be aware of that. When we got faster boats that made about 16 knots, we'd run them down. We'd come up on the whale and get him going, then sit right on top of his neck so he didn't get a chance to blow out or blow in. He'd start jumping because he couldn't finish his blow. He has to recharge his batteries, and you tire him out.

When we were after a whale, we were in high gear, excited. We were always waiting for daylight to come so we could get going, and dark came too soon. We didn't think of it as hard work; we were so keyed up by the excitement that time didn't mean anything anymore. As soon as that 180-pound harpoon gun went off, we were out of our bunks in a hurry. Sometimes the harpoon line caught around the propeller, and the whale would tow us, stern first. A dying whale often stands on his tail and goes in a circle. Once, we couldn't back away from a dying whale fast enough, so he came right in and landed on the winch in the middle of the boat. He flattened the whole rail and died right there—60-odd tons of whale.

If you're experienced in whaling, you can tell from miles off what kind of whale it is. The blow tells you. Humpbacks have a short, stumpy blow. A sperm whale's blow doesn't go straight up: it's flat, almost parallel to the surface. No other whale blows that way. The blue whale blows a big fountain: it spreads up and out. A finback's blow is more concentrated all the way up: it's more rounded and doesn't branch out. The sei whale has a thin, narrow blow. I've only seen two or three right whales in my whole career, so I can't tell about them.

A whale has a built-in barometer we haven't got, especially the humpback. He can sense a change of weather long before it

Humpback whale, Bonavista Bay

comes. He jumps over and splashes on his back, trying to get off all the barnacles, lice, shells and whatever else grows on him. We'd say, "He's cleaning himself," and we'd batten the boat down and prepare for a blow.

I had two whalers when whaling was banned in 1974. My living was taken away from me, and I didn't feel very good about that. I was only taking small minke whales, but they didn't differentiate between the species. The minkes are not an endangered species. Every part was utilized: the meat went to Norway and Japan; the blubber was rendered for oil and used in the manufacture of soap, medicine, paint, ammunition and other industrial applications.

Don't get the impression I love to kill animals; I don't. I hated to shoot every one I shot, but you can't let that control your business. You have to make a living, even if you don't like that part of it.

I never worked on the land for pay in my life.

Henry Mahle, retired whaling captain, Dildo

It was Ash Wednesday morning, 1942, the beginning of Lent. I was on my way from 9 o'clock mass to my job in St. Lawrence when I heard the news: "There's been a big shipwreck." During the early hours of the morning, the American destroyer *Truxtun* was wrecked in Chambers Cove near St. Lawrence. The *Pollux*, a cargo ship travelling in convoy, was also aground farther up the coast. There was a raging sea and a big storm of wind and sleet. Two sailors from the *Truxtun* had braved the sea and swum ashore. They somehow made it up the huge 600-foot cliff, stumbled into the Iron Springs Mine and alerted the miners.

People started rushing into our store, looking for soups and foods to give the survivors. We were in a state of shock. I went from house to house with a couple of girls, collecting clothes. Everybody gave whatever they had: the husband's only sweater, clothes off the line above the stove, blankets. Many a man came home that night and had no underwear to put on. People knew there were hundreds of young sailors out there, clinging onto the ships for their lives, and they were ready to give anything.

That year, my mother had given me a $5 box Brownie camera. I thought, "This is really history in the making. I wish I could get out there." But my brother, the assistant superintendent of the mine, was a very staid person. He never went one bit to the left; it was always to the right. I felt that if I went out there with a camera, he'd kill me for sure. I was 19, but in those days, we regarded older brothers as parents.

When he stopped at the house that afternoon, I was on pins and needles. I wanted to go out there so bad. He asked me why I hadn't gone.

"Because of you," I said. "I figured you'd have heart failure if I arrived on the scene with a camera."

"Well, child," he said, "you should've gone."

"Good enough," I said.

What greeted my eyes in Chambers Cove was the sight of sailors clinging to the sides of the capsized destroyer like flies clinging to honey. The waves were terrible, and the whole sea was covered with crude oil from the ship. It was one of those real winter storms, sleet and hail, and a terribly strong southerly wind was dashing right off the Atlantic at the shore.

Our men tried to rescue the sailors in every way. They tried to send a boatswain's chair and all sorts of cables to the ship, but the gale would take them. The only way the sailors could save their lives was to jump into the sea. The crude oil was as hard as tar and made it almost impossible for the poor fellows to swim. Some would get within a couple of feet of being pulled in, and a huge wave would come and take them out. That would be the end of them. I got pictures of our men pulling the poor fellows up the cliff. Some of them were too weak and had to be carried up; many were dead. I felt terrible, like crying. I felt as if something had happened to someone very dear to me.

The next morning, the scene was gruesome. The poor old ship was out there on her side, and the waves were battering against her. There was all kinds of salvaging going on by the Navy men who had arrived from the American base in Argentia. They tried to shush me away. I asked a young sailor, "What the heck is all the fuss about?"

"Confidentially," he said to me, "it's the decoder we're pulling up."

The man in charge came over and said, "I don't like you taking pictures right now."

"I'm a correspondent for *The Globe and Mail*," I said. It wasn't very smart because the news of the wreck was being kept secret, but he let me stay.

Two days afterwards, I got pictures of the *Pollux* farther up the shore. The next day, Sunday, she was gone. Throughout the week, I skied out to the wreck of the *Truxtun* and got pictures of the bodies hauled up the cliff and later of the funeral services in St. Lawrence. Vice Admiral Bristol, the commander of the base at Argentia, sent Lieutenant Commander McCaleb to ask me, as a personal favour, to release the film.

"No way," I said. "I'll never see my pictures again. When I get them printed, I'll send him a set."

"Miss Farrell," he told me, "you won't get them printed."

"I will, when the war's over. They are my pictures, and you're not getting the film," I replied.

The rescued sailors thought I was quite a hero to keep my film from the U.S. Navy.

About a week later, the Associated Press phoned and said if I'd release the pictures to them, they'd have them printed, use the ones they wanted and return all the others, prints and negatives. "Great God," I said. "Sure, I'll give them to the Associated Press."

Two weeks after that, I was right thrilled to see my pictures in the *Montreal Standard*, *The Globe and Mail* and *The New York Times*. I thought I was quite the photographer. I got a letter from one of the editors and $100 for the eight pictures he had used.

That $100 was a lot of money then, me a young girl. I invested it in a "616" folding Kodak that came out like an accordion: a $100 camera, and I was all set.

For months afterwards, there were bodies drifting in. Years after that, there was an awful lot of crude oil in the sand and we were always picking up pieces of sailor suits, collars and caps and old shoes.

Five years later, I got tired of office work, and since I had a lot of relatives down in New York, I decided to take a year off and go down there. I'd been corresponding with the wife of the Lieutenant Commander of the *Truxtun* because she was so genuinely grieved. I spent a week with her in Washington and photographed Arlington cemetery, where the bodies were brought back and buried, the Capitol building, the Supreme Court, the Tomb of the Unknown Soldier. I was thinking it would be a nice finale for my pictures—the whole story carried right through.

I came back to New York and took the subway to Brooklyn, where I was staying. I put the camera beside me, and when I got off at my stop, it was gone. There was nobody to ask. I have never felt so lost before. I rang "Lost and Found." They didn't know anything about it. Then I put a $15 ad in *The New York Times*, but I never heard anything.

I was so utterly disgusted. I thought, "Gee whiz, to hell with the big city. If that happened in our small town, within hours I'd have it; somebody would know where it was or who took it."

Ena Farrell Edwards

Ena Farrell Edwards, librarian, St. Lawrence

Frost in July

I cried and cried when I first came to Newfoundland.

I was six months pregnant, and we had taken the night crossing on the Port aux Basques ferry, sleeping on the floor. We woke at 6 o'clock in the morning and got off, knowing all our belongings were coming behind us. This was it.

There was ice in the puddles and snow in the woods. There was nothing green, just sheer rock. It was such a desolate place.

In Ontario, you complain about how cold the winter is and how awful the summer is, but here it's intensified. There's very little summer. Growth is a desperate process. Tonight, they're calling for a frost. This is the middle of July, the only month we normally don't have to worry about it.

Yet it's a calm place to live. At times I feel isolated, but mostly it just lets me be myself.

Shauna Steffla, artist, Corner Brook

Frost on window, François

Entrance to Rencontre Bay

Father

We had Father given up one time. It was the middle of winter. A storm had come up quickly, and by the end of the day, he hadn't returned. At 7 o'clock, our kitchen was full of people. The clergyman was there. The merchant was there. They seldom came to the house unless someone was dying. My mother was crying. My older sisters were crying. My uncle was there. The whole ritual. There was no way that Father could come out from that storm.

We heard pounding on the door and the door opening. In he came. He had a scarf around his neck. There was a great big lump of seawater that had frozen there early in the day, right under his chin, under his throat. He attempted to get the scarf undone. My uncle George reached over and took the bread knife off the table and just slid it down inside the scarf and said, ''You don't need that on any longer.'' The merchant passed him a flask of brandy: ''I daresay you could use a drop of this now.'' I was only 7 then, and it was one of the happiest moments of my life.

The engine had given out, and they'd landed their dory up off the old sandbanks. They'd fastened her down and had managed to walk overland through the storm and get into Burgeo that way. The next morning, they walked back and saved the fish. They didn't lose a single one.

They were very cautious men, the dorymen. They took good care of their boats and their engines. Their boats were tight all the time. Very few of them went down. Once the men went out to sea, that was it. They had no radios. Most of them refused to learn to swim. I remember asking my father about that. He said, ''If I go in that salt water, my son, the sooner the better for me.'' They were skilful and calm. They were not foolhardy men, and they had a lot of respect for the ocean. Sometimes, they got caught in bad weather, but they knew how to handle it. They could handle a boat on a wave as high as a house, taking it as it rolled in miles from land, coming down on it and floating just like a flower on the water.

Father didn't want me in a dory; he didn't want me to be a fisherman. He had seven daughters and only three sons. There were 15 at one time. Five died as children. I was well down the

Salmon catch, Conche

ladder, but my older brother got caught. There was no choice—
he had to help out. That's what sons were for.

Father went out even when other fishermen stayed in. He was
good. I know he was angry too. He recognized that his lifetime
of toil and skill had paid little reward in proportion to his efforts.
He questioned it and finally threw it up—that was the expression
he used—threw it up and left Newfoundland as an aged man in
his sixties. He ended up as a gardener in a hospital in Montreal.
He looked after the grounds. He was walking across the street one
November evening after his day's work when he was knocked
down by a motorcar and killed. A man who had survived the sea
all his life, killed by a motorcar in Montreal.

Yes, he questioned it. They all questioned it. I remember
sitting for hours in the kitchen listening to them. They were
bitter. They were angry. It was their thinking that led to the
labour movement and the Fishermen's Union in Newfoundland.

Clyde Rose, publisher, St. John's

Retired fishermen, Bay de Verde

Boats in an August snowstorm, Nain

A perfect out

While the Inuk appears to be extremely friendly and acquiescent, people who know anything about the Inuit culture will tell you it is a cover-up for fear too. This culture has a form of taboo on expressing anger and strong emotions. If you let them show, you'll be considered not terribly rational. If you hide these emotions, pressures will build up. Also, the missionaries in Labrador told the people countless times that if you drink, you get irresponsible. Don't drink, because you don't know what you are doing.

It's a beautiful out, a perfect out, because the Inuk then deliberately drinks to vent this pressure and, at the same time, does it without censure from his own culture: ''Rosie didn't know what she was doing.''

Tony Williamson, international development director, St. John's

Candy

Once there was a terrible flu epidemic in our Eskimo community of Okak. There was one small girl who survived. Martha was her name. A dog saved her. Other dogs ate the bodies of the people that died and tried to attack this little girl, but there was one husky who protected Martha and kept the dogs away from her. When people finally came, she was under that dog, keeping warm.

I am 92 years old. When I was growing up near Okak, we had some flu, but nothing like that. I was 4 years old when my own mother died. I cried some but didn't think about it after that. A Hebron couple took me in. They didn't hug me, but they never reprimanded me.

I liked having candy. The couple used to go away during the summer to hunt. After they left, I would wake up in the morning and put my hand under my pillow, and there was a candy. I enjoyed it. I could tell they really loved me. They could only get it when the supply ship came in.

Later, I was married but didn't have children, so I adopted a little daughter. I was married three times, the last time to Martin Martin, who became chief elder of Nain. I was "boss lady."

I had an eye disease when I was 25 or 30. A doctor came on a ship, and when I showed it to him, he took my eye out. Two of my teeth were aching all the time too, so the doctor took all of them out, instead of just the two. I was quite mad at him.

I liked to work best at sewing, with my thimble and my needle.

Susanna Martin, Inuit widow, Happy Valley

Susanna Martin, Happy Valley

Eaton's catalogue

I arrived in Cow Head in January of 1950, a year after Confederation brought Family Allowance and the Eaton's catalogues into the communities. Everyone was content until people saw the catalogues. We all had the same oilcloth on our tables. We all had flour-bag blinds. We didn't have any choice. We were limited to what was in the few stores in the community, unless we went to Corner Brook, and we only went to Corner Brook if we were sick and they couldn't help us at the cottage hospital. But when the catalogues came into the homes, we had a choice. We were able to sit down and see other things. It was just like heaven.

It was a whole new world. The women had a choice of dishes and curtain material. At first, it was only Christmas and Easter when we got things. Children would go together through the catalogue and say, ''We are going to get this dress for Christmas,'' and they would all pick the same clothes. People would ask each other, ''What page did you get that from?''

Hooking a rug, Cow Head

When a man brought home his paycheque, his wife used to put it in the cashbox. It wasn't hers, and she wouldn't make a purchase without his approval. But when the Family Allowance cheques came, they were always in the mother's name. That was her money to spend, and she could now say, ''We'll buy this for Christmas'' or ''We'll save up and get a gasoline washer.''

Through the catalogue, women gradually put things in their homes that they had never even known existed. But it was the road, built in the 1960s, that made us materialistic. People started travelling. They would come back and say, ''I think I want a rectangular, one-storey bungalow like the ones in Deer Lake, instead of a square house'' or ''They have carpets now in Norris Point. We're going to have carpets in Cow Head.'' But people didn't wish for something that they couldn't see.

Jane Hutchings, retired district nurse, Corner Brook

molasses and flour and put it in the oven. That's what the people called "lassy mogs."

There were eight of us. We'd all be around then and waiting for that to be cooked. She'd take it out and break it apart, and that's what we would have before we'd go to bed. Then in the morning, my poor old father and I left and went into the woods. And when it come time to boil the kettle, he'd take a slice of bread and break it in two pieces, and then he'd take that and bust it into four and burn it up and put it in our kettle. That's what we had for tea—burned-up bread. No molasses. And sugar? I hardly knew what sugar was.

There was food in the stores, but they just wouldn't let us have it because we didn't have nothing to pay for it with. Just what we would get for our fish, three-quarters of a cent a pound, salted. That was in what they called the Dirty Thirties. I heard that on television. The only thing that kept us alive was that we reared our own vegetables. But we had no pork or beef.

Jobe Symes, retired fisherman, Port aux Basques

Starvation

I only got grade four because I had to come out of school, owing to starvation. I used to wait for hours, hours and hours, for my poor old father to come with something to eat. He'd left and gone over to Rencontre, a place three miles from we. And in those days, they didn't call it relief, they called it dole. When he got back in the house, he had 12 pounds of flour and a quart of molasses. My poor old mother, she'd make up this water and

Tattoo, Signal Hill National Historic Park, St. John's

An emotional time

The time of Confederation was an emotional time all right. I know some people who flew their flag at half-mast on the anniversary of Confederation for many years afterwards, and on the day itself, many people pulled down their blinds in mourning. It was a very strong time. We were polarized. You were anti or pro, and there was no shilly-shally. You made your choice fairly early, and you stuck to it.

Aloyhius O'Brien, farmer, St. John's

Cove, Burgeo

Confederation

Personally, I don't regret the move of joining Canada one bit.

You think we're quaint now? We would've been pretty quaint if we hadn't.

Brian Walsh, mayor/fisherman, Bay de Verde

The trapper

In those days, we were all living off the land, and at times, it was hard for everybody to get a trap line. Some fortunate people had more than one, maybe handed down from another member of the family who had passed away. They would hire trappers to work their other lines.

Well, my trap line was 300 miles away, and one winter, a friend of mine offered me one a lot closer. When you take another man's trap line, you don't know where the route goes, where it crosses the brooks, how it crosses land. You have to blaze trees and watch yourself pretty carefully. This guy drew up a map for me, and it was very accurate. I had my dog Winsor with me. He was a thoroughbred husky and weighed about 100 pounds. He was the best watchdog and hunter I ever saw on four legs. He could smell his way on thin ice. By shimmering his nose down, he knew if it was thick enough. He was never scared of anything, including black bears, and that's rare in a dog.

I was following this trail—watching the map, crisscrossing the brook—and had come to where I had to cross a neck of land. It was getting dark, so I got a lot of wood cut and built a brush lean-to. I got in there beside my fire, and I roasted a partridge for my supper. I gave my dog a couple, raw.

My friend had told me he had seen a cougar a few times in this area. I was only 22 and not familiar with cougars. The only thing I had for a gun was a .22-calibre rifle, but I had killed every other animal I had ever seen with it and I felt pretty safe. I got everything straightened away and was lying back on my sleeping bag with a nice big fire going. I was almost asleep when, suddenly, my dog let out this big growl and bark all in one and came straight through the brush right on top of me.

He was really scared. His hair was all stuck up on his back, and he was shivering. I had never seen him scared in his whole life. I said, "What the hell is going on? There's something here that he doesn't know." I looked at the dog again. He was still trembling, right afraid. So I went over, picked up the gun, put a shell in the bridge and walked around to look behind the lean-to, where the dog had come from.

There were two big yellow eyes about 30 feet away, 4 feet off the ground. It looked like a damn good-sized animal. It had to be a cat. I tried to aim at him, but it was too dark. I tried to get my dog out alongside me, but he wouldn't move. It was the only time in his life he ever refused an order.

I backed off to get the light of the fire on my gun's sights. I took really good aim and pulled the trigger. The eyes disappeared, and I heard a big crash in the bushes. Sounded nice; sounded like I got it really good. I went to the fire, took a chunk of burning wood and swung it around to make it good and bright. I took my gun; the dog wouldn't come with me.

It was a great horned owl. He must have swooped on over the dog real close and scared him in his sleep, then landed on a low tree in the woods. I had hit him fair between the eyes. I picked up the owl, carried it back and heaved it on top of the dog. I told him off good. I said, "This is what you were scared of. You frightened the hell out of me." I gave him a real good tongue-banging, and he just put his head down and stared up at me. When I saw him looking scared and knew that he was apologizing, I put a smile on, and his face brightened up again. Just the same as a person would. But that was the biggest scare I ever got in my life.

Little scares? I've had lots of those. I fell through the ice a few times, and it looked serious, but the same dog helped me out. When I fell in, he saw what happened and came over. I said, "Down! Down!" And he got down on his belly, crawled right up to me and got hold of me with his teeth, behind the neck, making sure it was only clothing: my heavy jacket, shirt and heavy underwear. Then he backed off. He was a great help.

I can make a good bit of money at trapping. The way me and the wife lives, we don't need much money. Our biggest bill other than house needs is our phone bill—the children are strung across Canada and the States. Now when I go trapping, I usually only go for a week. With a snowmobile, I can cover 100 miles a day, which would take 10 days the old way. But I'd still like to go in sometimes for a couple of months, all by myself.

Horace Goudie, trapper, Happy Valley

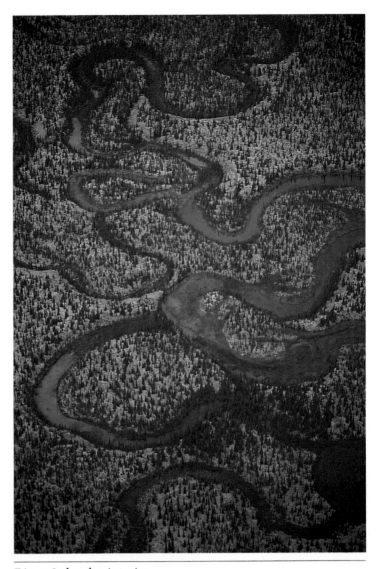

River, Labrador interior

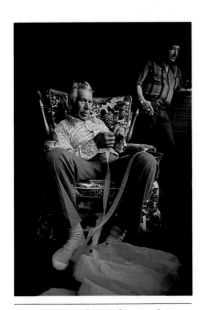

Horace Goudie, John Baikie

Sheep, Sally's Cove

Nippers and stouts

The first part of the spring, we have the nipper, the one that sticks his stinger down in you and sucks the blood out. He is a quarter of an inch long, has long legs and hums around your ears. After him, we get the black fly; he bites hard. Then we get the sand fly, the one you can't see. They make your skin go on fire, get in your eyes, make life very uncomfortable. Next, we get the stout. Now he is a much larger fly; he is as big as an old fish fly. He bites hard enough. We say he takes a piece out of you, goes up a tree and eats it. We always use some kind of fly oil. It runs down with your sweat and makes your eyes smert.

Esau Ings, lumberjack/fisherman, New World Island

Keeping warm

There was no central heating. You had a kitchen stove, and that was all. When the stove went out at bedtime, it wouldn't be lit again till 7 o'clock the next morning. It would become so cold the chamber pot would often freeze under the bed.

We used to get big beach rocks and leave them in the oven all day. In the evening, we wrapped the rocks in socks and put them in our beds. About 2 o'clock in the morning, there'd be a big bang as somebody's rock fell out of bed.

That was only 20 years ago.

Brian Walsh, mayor/fisherman, Bay de Verde

Girl and cat, Greenspond

When I was a young man, you could see real forest here. My father was manager for a district, and each district would have from 6 to 12 camps, and each camp would have about 50 men, with a foreman and a cook and horses. They would go in and start cutting, usually about the first of September when the inshore fishery was over. The men who had been at the fishery would get jobs for the rest of the fall until Christmastime, cutting the trees in 8- to 10-foot lengths and clearing away the stumps. When the snow was right, we'd go in with the horses and haul the wood down to the lakes or the river. It would stay there until the spring. Then about the beginning of May, the rivers would break up, and another gang of men would go back and throw the wood in the water, and it'd all float, helter-skelter, down the rivers.

We cut fir and black spruce. It was hard work, and there was good food too. I still don't know how the cook did what he had to do. The water had to be brought in buckets up from a pond or a brook, firewood had to be got, kerosene lamps filled and cleaned, the bunkhouses cleaned out, the floors scrubbed. Bread! The quantities of bread that those 50 men would eat, baked on those little old stoves.

Wages weren't very big. Two dollars a day when I started out, and on some jobs, less than that. I remember working on the river drive in spring and getting 17 cents an hour. We went on strike— we wanted 22 cents an hour. We were 20 miles up in the woods, but the men learned that we were supposed to be getting 22 cents. It'd been in the newspaper, and the rumour got around.

Black spruce, Gros Morne National Park

We downed our tools and marched down the river to meet the boss. The boss happened to be my father, so I wasn't one of the leading agitators—I wasn't Lech Walesa. My father came out to meet us and said he couldn't talk to a hundred men all at once, so we appointed two or three to talk to him in the cookhouse. My father had a sense of humour. They said they wanted 22 cents an hour, and they felt entitled to it. ''Nothing else now, are you sure you don't want something else?'' Oh yes, they said, they wanted to have prunes and dried apples included in the menu. He said, ''Well, I'll meet you halfway. I'll give you the prunes and dried apples, and forget the money.''

We ended up getting it all. We also got a lecture from my father, telling us that if working men kept on being outrageous in their demands, they'd have the mill in Grand Falls closed down, and nobody would have a job. The mill is still going, but some of the men are not.

There weren't any really big trees, but there wasn't all this tangle of brush and dead trunks. Today, they are just demolishing the woods. They don't clear up afterwards, which creates an

Fern, Gros Morne

awful fire hazard. Fires don't get started in nice tall groves with green moss all around.

We never did as much damage because it was all done by men and horses. Now they have big machines that cut the trees off and lay them down and these big-wheeled skidders that haul them out to a roadside. It's simpler for the big companies to buy these machines for half a million dollars than to hire half a dozen men, and what they can't do by machine, they don't do at all.

The paper companies are the culprits. They are not interested in management of the forest. I once said to the woods manager in Grand Falls, "How can you bear to do what you are doing, cutting little half-grown trees, destroying the woods? Twenty years from now, you will be wishing you hadn't done that." He said, "Look, Edgar. I'm only concerned about the profits and losses and the balance sheet of this company this year. As for 20 years from now, go and talk to somebody else. I'm not interested." And they're still not. Men became more greedy about wages, and the companies became more greedy about their profits. We're all to blame for that.

Edgar Baird, retired lumberjack/pilot/businessman, Gander

We was at the party. When we got back in the porch, the missus switches on the light and says, "Oow! Ooow!" And I says, "What the hell is wrong with you?" I thought it was a drunk or something on the floor.

Well, we've got this stuffed fox, and they'd put it at the door. The chesterfield was out there, legs up; the big chair, legs up; the table was in the head. Oh, what a going-on. We didn't mind, because it was only fun, eh? They never beat up nothing, tore up nothing, so I guess they had a good time for themselves while they were here. No hard feelings: it's only Christmas.

My missus had a bottle of pickled wieners. One keeps them for when one's going to have a party or something. They had one stick up over the weather glass, one in the fox's mouth, two or three on the floor. My wife says, "I wonder what's happened to the vinegar?" I said, "It's probably over at the sink."

Well, today she starts putting bread to rise. We have these two kettles on the stove, and she's always got them full of water. By God, that's where she discovered where her vinegar went. If she hadn't smelled it, we would have had vinegar bread.

I called Louis this morning, and I told him, "You'd better get up because you guys have to go to Burgeo on the boat now. I

Ruth Durnford, François

Santa Claus and children, François

called the Mounties, and they'll be waiting for you. And the
magistrate is coming down from Port aux Basques and going to
have a court. I'm taking you up for breakerage and entry, see?''

He says he never entered, just stayed on the porch, and the
others passed the whisky out to him. Just Christmas fun.
O-ho-ho!

Clyde Durnford, fisherman, François

You hook the quills and pluck them

We looked up to the Indians for a lot of things. They were a part of the land, you might say. We would talk to them and watch them working. They tried to learn something from us, and they were willing to teach us anything. It was easy to learn from them. I was a young fellow then, and they'd have all kinds of patience with me.

They would come out of the country in June, after breakup, and set up their tents in the old tradition, always the same area near North West River or Kenemich. They'd have their little places up in the woods where they would build or repair a canoe, make snowshoes or whatever they needed for the next winter's trapping. They'd stay there for about three months and see the priest every Sunday when they went to mass. By September, they would go back to the country.

There was one family that mixed well with my type of people—the Pasteens. When I was young, Michaud Pasteen and his brother camped not far from my trap line. They made it a habit

Rabbiter, Crabbes River Valley

to visit me each week. It was not to trade or anything like that, just to check. They had a lot of caribou killed, and every time they came, they would bring me this little bag of caribou meat, sometimes dried and smoked. They might pick up a porcupine or a few partridges for their camp on the trip over.

Michaud came one day and was watching me repair my snowshoes; my father had taught me how to do that. Michaud kept looking at my snowshoes and finally said, "Boy, they are bad.

You should have better snowshoes.''

"They'll last till I get home," I told him. About a week later, his older brother visited. We boiled the kettle and had a cup of tea. As he was leaving, I noticed an extra pair of snowshoes.

"You've got a new pair of snowshoes there, Simon."

"Oh yeah," he said. "They're yours. Michaud made them for you."

"But I didn't ask for any snowshoes," I said.

"No," he said. "But your snowshoes are getting awfully bad."

"But I've got no money either."

"Oh no, no money," he said. "That's a present."

There are many things Michaud taught me. He taught me to clean porcupines the Indian way. The first thing you do when you kill a porcupine is you bleed it, same as you would a pig. Put your knife down in the throat, down to the main artery in the heart, and just tip it upside down. The blood will come right out. When my father killed a porcupine, he would take out the insides right then and clean it that night or the next morning. The Indian way is you clean it with the guts still in. You cut a little tree, about three inches in diameter, at a comfortable height to work on. You sharpen it to a point with your axe. Take the porcupine, and ease the hole through which you bled it over the top of the stick, so it is hanging right there in front of you. With your axe—and you don't need it too sharp—you hook the quills and pluck them. You don't cut them. They're big, and you have to hook your axe in and pluck them right out. On the belly side, you singe the hairs. If you singe it with the quills on, you have too much of a smoky taste. The way my daddy used to do it, with the guts out first, the skin would draw and get wrinkly. The way Michaud taught me, the porcupine blows up naturally from the heat, and the belly is right smooth all over. It's easy to scrape clean with a knife. When it wrinkles, you get hair left in every wrinkle.

In the country, we would bake porcupines in a camp stove or cut them up in pieces and stew them with a little bit of fatback. They've a taste of their own—quite fatty, something like bacon—but those big old porcupines can be very tough and hard to cook.

Horace Goudie, trapper, Happy Valley

Children in sand dunes, Gros Morne National Park

The biggest kind of babies

You was worried from the time you got pregnant until the baby was born because you didn't know if you was going to live or die. There's the dread you lived in. We had our children in the homes with the old midwife. If you lived, you lived; if you died, you died. That's what you had to look forward to if you were a woman. Tough. There was nothing you could do.

And you'd work like dogs. Lug your water. Get down and scrub your floor. Scrub your clothes on the scrubbing board. Lift your washtubs in and out the doors. I done that when I was having my children. I had three. I washed and scrubbed the day before I had my last baby. I was feeling sick that day, but I got up and had to wash—I had two more small children. I washed the floor; I washed the children; I washed the clothes, emptied the washtubs out—everything. Women don't work now when they're going to have babies. They're frightened. They're miserable creatures. We had the biggest kind of babies and the strongest kind. Just like elephants. After the baby was born, you might stay in bed 10 days, but on the tenth day, you got up. You washed your baby, washed the baby's clothes, made the bread.

When the baby was sick, you treated it for what you thought was wrong. If the children had earache, their ears would turn red and they'd screech. Well, you'd know they had earache. When they was teething, there was nothing you could do. At nighttime, you'd sit up in bed and just seesaw all night long with the baby. It would cry, and you wouldn't know what's wrong. Nobody to bring the child to, to see what was wrong. When you've got a baby or a child and they're screeching a bomb and they can't tell you what's wrong, it certainly does something to you. It hurts you. I'd sooner be sick myself than my child sick.

There's the life we had. Then you say, "Love, how far will it fly?" You loved your children, but when you think back over your life now, what was there to love? Hardship, hard work. There wasn't much love in it. Then they leave when they get older. Nancy left when she was 16—went to Toronto. Bruce was 20 when he left and went training to be a nurse. But our other son, he always stayed here. He lived in this place. He's dead now— killed in an accident two years ago. He's got two kids down here.

Father and daughter, Ferryland

Nancy used to say, "Mum, George can't live without you and Dad." He stayed here, and he married here; he liked to be handy to Mum and Dad. He left us though, didn't he?

Hard to have them and harder to lose them too. That's the way it's all made up, isn't it?

Carrie Guinchard, homemaker, Hawke's Bay

When I first came to Newfoundland, I was prepared to love it because it was Christopher's, and I was completely "nutso" about Christopher. I thought it was the most beautiful place I had seen in my life. I have never been anywhere where the air was so clean, where vision was so sharp. Compared with New Brunswick, where I grew up and which has a haze over it all of the time, this place was brilliant.

I remember we went down to Placentia Bay and around the Cape Shore. We saw a funeral procession. The men carried a big cross and the casket, followed by mourners in black, all in the spring sunshine, contrasting against the brilliant green of the grass and the little white church on top of the hill. Later, we saw a wedding procession, which looked much the same, with a cross held in front, then the bride and groom and also little trees attached to fence posts, with ribbons on them. The magic quality of Newfoundland got my imagination.

Newfoundlanders were entirely different from the way I was brought up. We were taught: All things in temperance. Don't get too cross, don't get too happy, don't be too sad. Everything in the right proportion. But here, it was everything in excess. It was either a horrible day, or it was a beautiful day. People were either absolutely awful, or they were absolutely wonderful. They were really rich or really poor. I wasn't used to it; I'd never seen it before. And nobody wanted to change it. I found it very jarring. I found, in that sense, Newfoundlanders were extremely lazy.

I can't tell you how many things were a test for me. I couldn't settle down. I was in a state of constant confusion. Finally, when we did come to Salmonier to live, I truly hated Newfoundland. I was ripped away from my own roots, friends, relatives and the social life that I had grown up to expect. Had I stayed in Fredericton, I would have worked for the church, the hospital or the Girl Guide troop, since people I respected had done that and I'd been trained to do those things. Here I was, in outport Newfoundland, with a stove I didn't know how to light, with constant in-laws and no friends, no furniture—and not a hope of ever having any—and simply no place for me.

I just about went crazy. One day, the children were all asleep, and Christopher was in town. I had been reading about twins who talked to each other a lot. Suddenly, I thought they were talking to me, telling me how I should run my life. I couldn't make them stop. It was just terrible. I put the TV on, but they didn't stop. Finally I woke up the children and got myself together. Then I realized I was in a state of such heightened sensitivity that I had to do something or I would go mad.

I wanted to go back to painting, but I really didn't know what to paint. I knew colour; I could draw. In school, I was at the top of the class. But I would go to art galleries and nothing would turn me on. I understood what good literature was, but I didn't understand anything about vision at all.

Then one day I was doing housework, and I went in to make our bed. We had a homemade bed, with turned posts painted black. The sun was coming in through the window, just pouring in on this unmade bed. The pillows were scrunched in the middle, wrinkled. There was a big blanket that had been put in a washer by mistake and stuck in a dryer by double mistake, so it had this heavy quality to it. And white flannel sheets with a blue band. And there was a bedspread that I had dyed, sliding onto the floor.

I went in, and it was as if somebody had hit me right in my solar plexus. It was the most erotic thing I had ever seen. I had read literary work that affected me erotically, but never had I seen anything that affected me like that. I knew then how you had to feel about something if you were going to paint it. It was as if all the windows were open and all the doors were open. I was so lucky. Some people go through their whole lives, looking, and they never find it.

After I saw that bed, I saw thing after thing. I never questioned why. I never said, "This must fit into what I have done before. This must prove something." It was the wonderful beginning of a career.

I learned that many painters used photographs in their work—even Picasso. I began to take pictures of things as I saw them. One day our neighbour Ed said to me, "How about taking a picture of my moose?" So I went to his garage, and I expected to see the

animal hanging outdoors. Where was it? He said, "It's inside."
And he opened the door. There was this moose, split open and
bloody, hanging from the crossbars of his wrecking truck.

I was so disgusted, so affronted that he would show me
anything so awful and not know what he was showing me. To
my credit, I didn't throw up or faint or do any of the usual
feminine things. While I was photographing, he kept saying,
"Do you want me to shove the legs farther apart? Do you want
me to move the crowbar around?" This was everything that man
does to women, that man does to nature. It was just horrendous,
the legs spread and held out in this almost clinical atmosphere,
with all these mechanical things governing the hopeless body.

Many years later, we lost two of our children. Our son John
became very ill. I grew up more. I thought that perhaps I could
do the painting. It took me about a year. When I finished it, I
phoned Ed and I said, "You want to come up? I finally did that
moose." So he came and looked at it and said, "Well, well. There
is my old truck."

Newfoundland presented me with things to paint—the fish,
the cruelty, but also an understanding of the basic, which I would
never have found in Fredericton. Everything stripped right
down: true joy, real hate, no apologies. Nobody apologizes for
hating anybody here.

I think that if I hadn't been brought to this terribly lonely place,
I wouldn't have been a painter at all. I wouldn't have seen
anything. I would have married a lawyer and had an ordinary
life. If I hadn't got stuck here, I probably wouldn't have ever
amounted to anything. If you are not stuck in a place where
everything you ever thought is questioned, you don't have to
think about it.

I feed off this land. It's beautiful, but I don't want to ruin it for
myself by painting it. My images spring from Fredericton. My
sense of order, my sense of colour. My work speaks of a
childhood in a cathedral town, with lawns and gardens and the
brilliance of autumn, and of my refusal to paint raw, bare things.
Everything has to be rich, encrusted with life and colour, like
jewellery. It has to show the passionate love of what I see.

Mary Pratt, painter, Salmonier

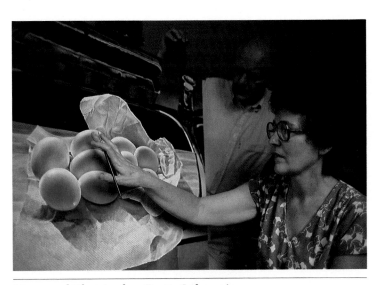

Mary and Christopher Pratt, Salmonier

Lobster Cove Head lighthouse, Gros Morne National Park

Edge of the sea

The sea defines the land; the sea is its edge, its boundary.

That's where you sense the land best, from its edge at the sea.

The sea around Newfoundland is not always rough. It can be tranquil and very brooding. To me, a real Newfoundland day is a still, grey day, as opposed to a stormy day or a sunny day. A still, brooding sea has a sense of power, of presence. In most places, the sea is very deep. The rocks roll down into it. It is cold; as soon as you're near it, you feel the cold coming up. It smells, because of the tides, the seaweed, the plants and animals. The water is clean and very fresh, seemingly unaltered, primaeval and untouched—which is not true, but this feeling is still there, because unlike the land, the sea seems unchanged.

Phillip Pratt, architect, St. John's

Capelin

A week ago, I saw some capelin, some numerous lot. I went out there, out to the saltwater. As far as I could see—up that way and down that-a-way, up on the sand, right along the land, 25, 30 feet wide—there was a foot of capelin, as far as I could see.

They say they are a one-year fish. They do not live two years or three. They comes to the land and spawns, then they dies. They don't lie very long on the sand with the sun. They dries up. At top high water, the sea shifts the sand and covers them in. You walk along there now, and your feet will feel it right soft, the spawn in the sand, down about two inches.

They claim that after a while, the spawn will wash out over the sand, into the sea, go off on the bottoms . . . little fishes next year, or whatever.

Lawrence Gibbons, retired fisherman, St. Vincent's

All my family were Confederates from 'way back. In 1869, one of the leaders of the Confederate movement, Sir Ambrose Shea, was going around the coast on a steamer. He came into Placentia and went ashore on the Southeast Arm. A mob got together, and they were going to hang him.

My ancestors lived across the harbour in the Northeast Arm. Eight of them came down in a skiff, with one of my great-aunts steering. They beat their way in, grabbed Sir Ambrose and put

him, trembling, back on the steamer. "How am I ever going to repay you for this?" he asked. And my grandfather said, "Why don't you build us a road up to the Northeast Arm?"

About two weeks later, a fellow came on horseback, and he had $650. That built the first road up there. There are pieces of it left, and every time I pass by, I think of that story.

After the second war, Confederation became an issue in Newfoundland again. I started to write letters to *The Telegram*, signed "Housewife." Joey Smallwood soon learned it was me. We got together and made a deal. I was the written word; he was the spoken word. He was good at that. About 60 percent of Newfoundlanders couldn't read or write, so he used to repeat everything in simple terms. He used to say, "You don't say to them, 'It's a black cat.' You say, 'It's a B-L-A-C-K cat.' You say, 'It's a B-L-A-C-K C-A-T. It's a black cat.' By that time, they should understand." It was very tiresome later, as people became more knowledgeable.

I became editor of the paper, *The Confederate*. There were no roads to most of the outports then, so we would fly over and drop copies into the communities. Sometimes we would land, and Joey would get out on the pontoon and talk by the public wharf. He used to say, "My dear friends, I have come to you out of the clouds." They didn't see anything wrong with that.

The Snows, Conception Bay

Winnie Parsons, Glenburnie

They were simple, honest people, poor and isolated. They didn't have any expectations. Infant and child mortality was awful. Diphtheria and tuberculosis were rampant, and since cousins married cousins, many were retarded. At the time of Confederation, the average life span was 48 years. Now it's 74 and going up.

The Catholic Church came out vehemently against Confederation with Canada. No one to this day knows why, except that the Church always supported the Establishment. Water Street businessmen were madly against it. Most of the professional people were against it. The paper companies in Grand Falls and Corner Brook poured in their money against it since they had gotten a sweetheart deal when they came here and weren't paying corporate taxes. After Confederation, the first ones they paid amounted to $3½ million each, so imagine what they took out of here in the previous 50 years. The colonial attitude has always been to suck out the blood, then leave without putting anything back.

During the referendum campaign, my wife's first cousin, a Crosbie, came out in favour of union with the United States. Many people looked upon the States as the land of milk and honey. When the price of salt codfish went down to the floor after the first war, the exodus to the States from places like Placentia Bay was enormous. House after house, everybody was gone. Those who went sent back money to relatives.

Many people who voted for responsible government and against Confederation thought they were voting for union with the United States, but it could never have happened. England was the most reliable ally that the United States had, and although the empire was falling, the Americans weren't going to offend her by taking over Newfoundland. The idea of union with the States wasn't even on the ballot paper, yet you couldn't explain to people that since it wasn't on the ballot, it couldn't be. We won Confederation, but if it hadn't been for that, we would have won by a landslide.

It was a revolutionary period in Newfoundland's history. For once, the multitude won against the Establishment.

Gregory Power, retired politician, St. John's

Joey and I

I was Newfoundland's Minister of Finance for five years. I had a continuous battle with Joe, who was always looking for the money, and I wouldn't give it to him. I'd go to bed with everything balanced and wake up in the morning with Joe on the phone, demanding $365,000 for a very worthy thing we should do. And I'd say, "You can't get it."

He'd say, "Why can't I get it?"

"Because it would eat up the whole estimated surplus."

"Who gives a goddamn about the surplus, besides you?" he would grumble.

We had $42 million that the Commission Government had saved up, which was a lot of money then, but there were 1,300 settlements when we took over. Should we try to bring them medical and dental services? Education? But who would go to all these isolated places?

It was impossible to bring them all anything worthwhile, so we decided to break the isolation. In the first 10 years, we built 4,000 miles of new road. We built the Trans-Canada out of St. John's, out of Gander, Grand Falls, Corner Brook and Port aux Basques. As we went, we changed the face of Newfoundland forever. Then came the schools, the university, the Arts and Culture Centre and hundreds of water and sewer systems.

When we built the roads, Joey used to say, "If we don't open them officially, we won't get the credit." Each community always had a big meal cooked for us. They'd be so delighted. They'd want to touch us. No one had done anything for them for 400 years. We felt for them, otherwise we wouldn't have done what we did. We could have done other things with the money.

The way it was in Newfoundland, you grew up and died in a little place and your world was about 30 miles in diameter. There's a nostalgia people get for places like that, and they grieve when they have to leave them, but their children would never go back there. Now their sons and daughters are getting degrees, and that's a good thing.

It was probably the best period of Newfoundland history. The changes were monumental. Joe stayed in power for 23 years—that's how the Newfoundlanders took to him. But one thing was

Joey Smallwood, Holyrood

noticed: we'd take nice people, elevate them to positions of authority, and overnight, they'd change into real sons of bitches.

Joey became quite a dictator too. I remember that in the House of Assembly, a fellow would get up to answer a question, and Joe would say, ''Sit down. I'll answer it.'' He tried that on me one day. It was after lunch, and he'd been drinking wine. I said, ''Mister Speaker, I have the floor; he has no right to interrupt me.'' And the Speaker was up there between us, sweating something awful.

Finally, Joe sat down, and I said to him, ''Now don't ever try that again, unless you want those snaggleteeth you have removed quickly.'' He never tried it again, but things didn't get better, so I resigned.

Years later, when he was defeated, Joe sent a member of the Cabinet to call a truce. ''Will you bury the hatchet, or are you going to take it with you to your grave?'' he asked me. But Joe wouldn't do it quietly. He had a testimonial dinner at the Newfoundland Hotel, and this was where we buried it.

Joe had a good intellect, although it wasn't a finely tuned one. He couldn't write poetry, but he could write wonderful political propaganda. Directly and indirectly, Joe was responsible for putting more food on more tables, more clothes on more backs and more hope into more hearts than any other man in Newfoundland history. He was the closest friend I've ever had.

Gregory Power, retired politician, St. John's

Family group at Inuit wedding, Nain

Camelot

No matter how wonderfully happy you might be, there are days when it comes barrelling down on you like a 10-ton truck: "I miss home. I want to be there."

I never ever got over that homesick feeling, that need to be here. There is an old saying, "You can take the girl out of Labrador, but you can't take Labrador out of the girl." And that is true. Coming home after 10 years in the States, I feel like a whole person; my spirit is intact.

But the family today is not as close as it used to be. When my parents were growing up, there was a communal sense of living. Brothers all worked the same fishing spot, trapped the same hunting ground and depended on each other in ways you don't depend on anybody today because technology and change have taken care of that. People are more concerned about what each individual is doing and not about what the collective is doing. They don't seem to be as necessary to each other.

You never heard of a person my mother's age being born in a hospital. Now, there's a ban against midwives. Today, women have to go to a hospital to have their children. They leave their communities, their husbands, their mothers and all those people who would give them support. There is something so cold about a big hospital and going through that experience with strangers.

You worked all week, and on Sunday, you visited your neighbours, often going down the coast in a boat. But people don't visit anymore. They have company right there in their sitting rooms: the box. Television offers good education and entertainment, but I hate it.

My family moved to Goose Bay when I was 4, but I would spend vacations on the coast with my paternal grandparents, who lived in Packs Harbour in the summer. My sister and I loved it out there. When we landed, we were greeted so affectionately by our grandparents, but for the rest of the summer, we had total freedom. The whole island belonged to us, and we could explore it from the moment we woke up till when we went to bed. It was the kind of freedom that Peter Pan and his band must have known or the Labradorian version of Camelot.

Barbara Wood, social worker, Happy Valley

Newly wed Inuit couple, Nain

The vote

Newfoundlanders don't see themselves as part of Canada.

They were sold down the drain. The vote was switched. They didn't vote to join Canada at all. A lot of the votes were taken by telegram. I heard that people who wanted votes for Confederation were going around getting names off gravestones. Since you could only get to many of these small settlements by sea, there was no way of proving it. Still, it came out in favour of remaining a colony, and the governor ordered the vote to be switched.

He was a British governor. The socialist government in England was appointing very funny people throughout the Empire at that stage. England had no money; the war had totally exhausted every single resource. Canada offered to lend England money if she would facilitate Newfoundland joining Canada, and the governor was promised that he'd be made a baron if he got rid of Newfoundland.

He could just see this slipping by, so he ordered the vote switched and was made a lord.

Lady Jacqueline Barlow, St. John's

Nelly Carter, St. John's

The Narrows of St. John's

Truckloads of money

Politicians like to believe that anything good happens because they voted for it in the House, that it's their political skill. And they've convinced many people that it's so. They haven't taken credit for inventing television or anything like that yet, but when they tell you about the things we didn't have 50 years ago, they try to indicate that the good that's happened in the meantime is because they're smart fellows and we were smart enough to vote for them.

After the war, politicians were going around putting a $10 bill under a poor man's nose, saying, ''Vote for Confederation now, and you'll get one of these every month.'' It was sheer bribery. I voted for Confederation myself, with my tongue in my cheek. I didn't believe in it then, and I don't believe in it now. We should've been on our own, the same as Iceland. The Ottawa people are giving us money now. They're sending it in truckloads. But at the same time, they're demoralizing our people.

Edgar Baird, pilot/businessman/retired lumberjack, Gander

Western Brook Pond, Long Range Mountains, Gros Morne National Park

Earache

My father used to smoke a pipe. When I'd get an earache, he'd put a bit of rag over the end of his pipe and get it going good. Then he'd blow down through the bowl, blowing the hot smoke through the stem into my ear. If it was too hot, I'd draw clear. I'd push a bit of cotton tow in on top of that. After a little while, my earache would ease.

My father did that for me lots of times.

Rufus Guinchard, fiddler, Hawke's Bay

When we left Newfoundland, it was a place to be rid of. It was a poor country, and my mother wanted us to go somewhere and be somebody. She was a Salvation Army officer, and she was hired to go to Toronto.

I returned when I was 28 and went back to Exploits Island, where I grew up. This was at the end of the resettlement programme, and people were leaving the island. There were a lot of tears and frustrations and fear. People were told by the government that they were inferior and that they should move to "growth centres" to educate their children. They were told they were poor compared with people in downtown Montreal or Toronto. I didn't remember them being poor. Poverty didn't exist on our islands because everybody looked after everybody else. If a man had a bad season, the community would help out.

But the women bought the official line; they wanted the better life. Men wanted to stay: this was their life—everything they owned was there. Eventually, the government forced people out by paying some of them off and taking out basic services. Once they were gone, the island was finished.

Poverty and other deprivations only exist if you recognize them. If we continue to believe we are the poorest province, we'll always be the poorest province. We are what we believe we are. If we could convince others that we're not poor, that we're very rich and fortunate people, it would show in our economy.

There is a lot of narrow-mindedness in small communities, a lot of jealousy that holds Newfoundlanders back. When someone starts to climb the ladder, people try to bring him down. They want everybody in the community to be the same. At the same time, there is a greatness about them: they are natural, creative, inventive people who deal with the realities around them, who live in the landscape easily.

Things are so real here. People are real. The landscape is real: harsh, beautiful, ugly. The rocks are like bones sticking out of the ground, with this thin skin of soil. They are always underfoot, and you are aware of them all the time. Wherever you go, the landscape and weather are overbearing. Fishermen are always on that edge, working between life and death. Out on the sea, there is death all around you but also life, because that's where you get your living from.

We are very realistic about death. We laugh at death. A lot of traditional jokes are about it, because death is always so obvious. Growing up in Newfoundland, you are faced with death; people die, and there they are, in their houses, for all to see. As a child, I remember my mother had to bury these people, and I always had to go and see their bodies laid out on the kitchen table, scrubbed and clean in a nice pine box, and mourners standing around at the wake, some crying, some getting drunk.

Every day, things would die. We would kill animals, kill fish, kill our favourite pig, our good cow. Small children died too. There was death all around us. Today, people are protected from that reality. There are hospitals and funeral homes. We buy meat all packaged up—it doesn't even look like an animal. But our reality is still reflected in attitudes, in music, in religion.

Religion has always been important in Newfoundland. That's what held people together, that common belief in God. But the church has always avoided anything to do with our real culture. You only see the Holy Land depicted in religious paintings. And when I was asked to paint the *Last Supper* in a Newfoundland setting for the Mary Queen of the World church, I used my friends—all fishermen's sons—as models. Many of them have contributed to the Newfoundland culture: there are painters, poets, a publisher. I had always wanted to bring the Newfoundland culture into the church, and this was my way of doing it.

For my paintings of the *Stations of the Cross*, I chose an old road in Portugal Cove and marked my stations there. You can follow this trail right along the edge of the cliff. At first, some parishioners were upset about putting Christ in the fishing shed, but they finally accepted it. We identify with our landscape, and these boats and fishing sheds reflect who we are.

I used myself as the Christ figure. I am also the executioner. In this duel between sympathy and a sense of guilt, I point the finger at myself.

Gerry Squires, painter, Holyrood

Fish killer

My father took the knife, and then I knew he was going to kill the whale.

My father, Gus O'Flaherty of Conception Bay, was 75 and still active in the salmon fishery. For years and years, whales, finbacks and especially porpoises have been a great curse for fishermen in Conception Bay. Nets are expensive. A salmon net can cost $300 or $400.

I would go in the summer and help. That morning, we went out. There were a lot of whales around, and there was a whale in my father's salmon net. It had torn about 25 fathoms of twine and had wrapped itself thoroughly in it. It was bleeding profusely. Most whales I've seen in nets drown because they get tangled up as they go down and get wrapped around the mooring, but this one had managed to stay alive. His breathing hole was just above the water as it ebbed and flowed. The flippers were severely cut. He was pretty peaceful. He seemed almost dead.

I said, "Dad, let's not kill him. Let's cut him loose." I guess I'd been softened by all this talk about whales. It took about half an hour of the most delicate work, cutting around the twine. It's really hard to get a whale out of a net when it's so tightly wrapped. There was blood all over our arms, inside our shirts, on our faces. He stayed on the surface for about five minutes, then

Windsurfing with humpback whales, Bonavista Bay

swam away. He was such a powerful animal, he could have just flipped the boat over.

It was a big event for my father because he's ordinarily quite brutal in his handling of whales. For me too. My father then said that it was time to give up fishing. I wrote a short story about it. It's called *Fish Killer*.

Patrick O'Flaherty, writer/professor, St. John's

Fairies

My grandmother went to her grave believing in spirits. She knew people who had been carried away by fairies and came back possessed. If someone fell off the cliff, the fairies did it. If someone got lost in the woods or drowned in a pond, the fairies did it. Everything was attributed to the unknown.

When we were young, Mother would see to it that if we went up on the hill on a foggy day, we had a bit of bread in our pockets to feed the fairies so they wouldn't spirit us away. It was also a good way to get children to come home at night. That stuff was very real to us.

I never heard of anyone referring to ghosts; it was always spirits and fairies. Protestants didn't seem to be affected by these apparitions. It was an Irish Catholic belief.

If somebody heard the "old hollies"—mournful cries made by dead fishermen floating in a dory and wailing an old chantey—he

Kittiwake colony, Cape St. Marys

knew that a big breeze of wind was coming. I remember my grandfather walking into a house and saying, "You can pull your boats in; I just heard the old hollies." And the men went down and pulled up the boats. Today, we never whistle when we are on the sea. It brings the wind.

On All Souls' night, we never threw the dishwater out the door because the lost souls were wandering the roads and we might soak them. We would leave the cover off the water barrel so they could have a drink. If we came home after dark, we didn't walk in the middle of the road but stayed close to the fences, groping along in the pitch black, hand in hand. We knew that night the souls had the right-of-way.

Back in my father's youth, there was a priest who was also a faith healer, but one night, he met the devil. It was wintertime, and a blizzard was on. The priest had gone to Red Head Cove to administer the last rites to a dying man. On the way back, he got lost and decided to stay by a big rock till daybreak. Suddenly, a black cat came out of the snow and looked at him. He knew it was the devil, so he quickly made the sign of the cross, and the cat went away. It soon came back as a black dog—a bigger devil. Eventually, the sign of the cross worked, and the dog vanished, only to return as an even bigger dog. This time when the priest made the sign of the cross, the devil growled. The priest had the Blessed Sacrament with him, and when the dog bit him on the hand, he touched it with the Communion host. The devil disappeared in a ball of fire.

The priest's hand never healed, and my father, an altar boy, often saw this big, oozing lump. My grandmother told me this story in all seriousness. In those days, we thought old people never lied. I don't know if today those associated with Ronald Reagan would agree with that. But I was 8 years old then, and terrified.

Brian Walsh, mayor/fisherman, Bay de Verde

Brian Walsh and son

Arm wrestling, Wabush

Success

When we moved into Mud Lake, there was no livestock, only a bunch of mangy dogs running wild. Now we have ducks and geese, rabbits, chickens, goats, guinea fowl and pigeons. They are supposed to help us maintain a certain life style and provide us with fresh meat and fresh eggs.

I remember when we came here first. I would walk down the river from Happy Valley to Mud Lake on a weekend, carrying a dozen eggs in my sack, and by the time I got home, they were solid lumps of ice. I figured I was going to change that, so I got myself a bunch of chicks.

It was the nicest thing to see those young hatchlings. We waited 20 weeks to grow them up, and the day my wife found the first egg, this was a sensation. This was success. And to see my children put on their rubber boots and go into the henhouse and take out the eggs they wanted for breakfast, this was again success. You can measure success in very small portions—the size of an egg.

Hans Felsberg, blacksmith/farmer, Mud Lake

Phoebe Rich, grass weaver, Happy Valley

Cemetery, François

Jannys

You get foolish when you get so old. But I enjoy that. You look forward to Christmas, to the 12 nights when you go jannying every night. Mummering, some calls it, but we calls it jannying.

One night, I said to Mike I was going to my friend's place and if any jannys came, to let them in. He said, "Indeed I won't. They'll only come in to see what kind of paper you've got on the walls or what you've got on the floor or what you got for Christmas." I said, "What of it? Let them come on in." "Go on," he said. "I'm not going to let any jannys in."

Well, Mrs. Slade and I got rigged up and went jannying. I got rigged in a man's combination underwear, and my friend got a nightdress and put that on. We went all down the road, and when it was time to come home, we came here and knocked to the door and Mike came out. We asked, "Is Mary in?" That is my name—Mary. He said, "No, she's gone out next door somewhere." We said, "Can we come in?"

"Oh," he said. "Yes, come in. She's likely to be here any time now."

So we came in and sat down. He didn't know us. And I looked at the wallpaper and said, "Oh my, ain't that a beautiful pattern." By and by, I looked at the floor. "Oh," I said. "What a canvas. That's a beautiful pattern." Anyhow, we went.

About 10 minutes later, I came in in my regular clothes.

"Mary," Mike said. "You just missed them."

"Missed who?" I said.

"Jannys."

"You don't mean it," I said. "I wished I had of been here. Who were they?"

"I don't know who they were," he said. "But whoever they were, they sized up the place pretty good. They looked at your nice paper and your nice canvas. What did I tell you!"

I died, but I didn't want to tell him.

The next day, we were talking about one thing and another and I said, "Go away with it. That was Ann and I last night."

And you know what he said? "How damn funny ye are."

I got a kick out of that.

Mary Jo O'Keefe, great-grandmother of 17, Carbonear

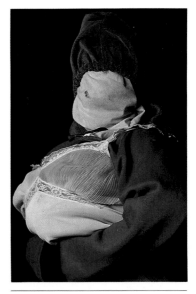

Mummer, François

Slowly died away

The hardest part was leaving. I kept thinking how foolish I was, and I'd just cry. The special things I had, I just put them in the fire and burnt them. The rest is still there. There was a sitting room off the kitchen; it was just to look at, really. There was a couch and a little cabinet—with china in it and photos along the top—made by someone in the harbour. Upstairs, there were three bedrooms. Parents had one, and the youngsters bundled up in the others, two or three in a bed.

At our wedding, we had every girl and every man—the whole harbour. I had a long dress; it came out of one of the catalogues. I asked for blue, but they sent pink, of all colours. We had liquor smuggled from St. Pierre. It was the end of August, a beautiful fine night. The next day, it was rainy. There were about 200 people, 40 families. Everybody was one another's neighbour; everybody would help one another. Even today, I look back on it and can see that it was more peaceful than it is around these bigger settlements.

It slowly died away. The first people started leaving about 1968, and we left in 1972. In the end, there were only eight families left, and we all went together.

Pearl James, formerly of Parsons Harbour

The Arches, northwest coast

Getting older

When I was young, I had to learn to catch the rabbit if I wanted to have rabbit soup for my supper on a cold evening in the fall of the year.

But when I got older, life changed. Now, if I comes across a live rabbit in my snare, I lets him go. A dead one, I puts him in my bag and takes him home, but to a live one, I says, ''Here, if you're man enough to go, go.''

Is it because I'm getting older, or is it because there is not the same need?

Joseph O'Brien Sr., retired fisherman, Bay Bulls

Flower girl, River of Ponds

Wild animals have a common trait: they don't like men or other animals in their territory, but they'll tolerate almost anything as long as they've had exposure to it, so the whale release procedure is a process of habituation. My strategy is to let the whales hear and see everything I do. I show them my equipment, and since the major stimulus of their fear is my boat and engine, I spend a long time approaching them. I think, "If I were to hunt this whale, what would I do?" and then I do exactly the opposite.

I think about whales as cows, huge herbivores that have few enemies and many friends. They swim along, munching on capelin, and are pretty laid-back. But humpbacks exploit the same niche as a fisherman with his cod trap; they are his direct competitors. Their skin is full of lumps and barnacles, so when they come close to a net, they tend to hang up.

It's the young whales, roaring around like teenage drivers, that end up in the fishing gear. We get only one or two big whales entrapped each summer, but you can argue that the big ones are just so goddamn strong they pass right through the nets. We don't know. For every whale that hangs up, there are probably three that just damage the net, so I only help in a small percentage of cases, but they're the bad ones. Last year, we released about 40 humpbacks, the year before that, 55, and about a dozen minkes each year.

After they are caught, they're relatively calm. Whales are so big and strong, they're their own worst enemy. If they turn their strength full on, they can really hurt themselves. The humpback's strategy seems to be, "When in trouble, lay back a bit, think about it, do nothing and things might get better." But nobody knows much about whales.

Once in a while, whales do unexpected things. We've only had one right whale entrapped, and because they're so rare, it's imperative that we try to save every animal. Rights are huge—70 tons, compared with 40 for a humpback. This one would swing his tail at me and lunge, although he had a whole cod trap wrapped around him. I asked the Fisheries for a bigger boat, and I tied a two-inch nylon braid—enough to tow an oil rig with—around his tail. We put it on the winch of a 55-foot seiner, winched the tail out of the water, and I was in my Zodiac boat ready to take the gear off, when the whale went under the hull of the seiner and raised it. I could see daylight under the keel. During the night, we lost him; I'm sure the whale died eventually. The young fisherman lost his only cod trap. That was the worst—just total defeat.

They're incredibly powerful. One time, I had a whale caught in a net and needed to tow him into a calm place so I could get the fishing gear off him. I tied one longliner to him; I couldn't pull him. I tied two longliners to him; I still couldn't. I tied three, but when he wanted to go the other way, he simply pulled these three large boats backwards. Somehow, we got him close to shore. I couldn't release him that night, so I tied a thick line to the gear wrapped around him and fastened it to a big rock. The next morning, the whale had broken loose. We had to take the three boats out again and tow him back in. Finally, on the third day, I literally beached the whale, removed the gear in one minute flat and pushed him back into the water with my boat.

We trailed the whale, wanting to stay with him for a while. He was swimming fast, flat out, near the surface. The fishermen were happy, even though he had cost them so dearly. They were saying, "Boy, isn't he happy to be free? Look at him go."

I knew that during those three days, they were often thinking of killing him, of making the bastard suffer for what he did to them. When an iceberg gets in their nets, they don't get emotional about it because there's nothing they can do with ice. With a whale, there is: they can kill him. Their nets were in one large knot, five feet in diameter and wound as tightly as a golf ball. If they were my nets, I'd have poured gasoline on them and burnt them, but the fishermen were delighted to have them back.

They were terrific men. Dirt-poor. The Great Northern Peninsula is not an easy place to live, but they had beautiful kids and all kinds of talents—the way these men often do. They accepted me as a peer, which I consider an honour. We had worked together, and these men made it good.

Fishermen don't like whales, and they'll never like them, but since I started the release programme in 1978, they've been magnificent. My job is to understand their feelings and accept them as perfectly legitimate. From their point of view, humpbacks are not an endangered population. ''We've got enough now,'' they say. But people in New York and Toronto don't have any idea that there could be too many whales.

I am also a scientific advisor to the conservation groups. It is very difficult, but I don't take sides. When I meet with fishermen, I always imagine there's a Greenpeace guy among them, an archetypal radical conservationist. When I talk to conservationists, I pretend there's a Newfoundland fisherman there. This helps me not to talk out of this or that side of my mouth.

I get mad at whales too, just like the fishermen. They are pests. They are like huge marine rats. I know that a cod trap costs $5,000 to $8,000 and takes several months to make. I know these men and their families, their life. These are people who in one month must harvest most of their earnings for a year, and these big bastards come in and foul it all up.

When I release whales, I try to do three things: save the whales, salvage as much of the gear as I can and teach the fisherman so he can do it himself in the future. After a whale is released, we relive the whole incident: ''And then his big black tail came up, swinging . . .'' That's the way we tell stories in Newfoundland. I start and prime them, but they set the parameters of the story. Then they go home and tell it to their lady, to their old man and to their kids. It's important: it validates the experience, and it encodes the techniques for keeping safe during the whale release and minimizing damage to their gear.

Releasing trapped whale, Jon Lien

They always react the same way the first time we're on the back of a whale. They turn around with this shocked reaction written across their faces: ''Holy Cow, will I live through this?'' They can't believe it. The second time, they turn around, and there is still anxiety, but then they smile. Every time, when we're done, the first thing they say when they come back to the wharf is, ''I was up on the back of a whale.''

That's it. They forget about the thousands of dollars they've lost, they forget their anger and fear, but they remember they were in a boat on the back of a whale.

Jon Lien, professor of animal behaviour, Portugal Cove

Streets of St. John's

St. John's

St. John's is an old city. For European mariners, it was by far the closest place to establish a convenient port for cross-Atlantic voyages. It's a well-sheltered place, a good harbour. If a harbour is too big, you get winds and waves, and if it's too deep, it's hard for boats to moor and anchor. Hundreds of schooners used to crowd the harbour, carrying all items of trade, not just fish but coal and salt and lumber and building materials and tea.

The harbour and the hills strongly determined the form of the city. The streets descending to the water's edge were actually small riverbeds and footpaths. Water Street is the oldest commercial street in North America, and the best side was always the south side with its access to the sea. This is where the most prestigious buildings, department stores and warehouses were built, with small wooden wharfs extending into the harbour. The north-side buildings were smaller—professional and service-oriented offices with some residences. Streets parallel to the harbour were more desirable. They were wider and, because they ran across the hillside, were easier to build on and more accessible to horse carriages. This early pattern still exists in St. John's, almost like the rings of a tree.

After Confederation, the development of the city went over the hill and into the valley beyond, where the university buildings, shopping areas and the airport were built. For the first time, the harbour lost its dominance; all of a sudden, communication by road with the rest of the island became the driving force for the growth of the city. It caused a lot of decay and lack of interest in the downtown. But now, big commercial buildings are returning to the harbour, the psychological centre of St. John's. They are as good as these buildings usually are, but the centre is too congested by the tight geography of water and hills for them to function properly. These new structures really have changed the scale of downtown, which, with its two- and three-storey texture, had a certain human scale and quality.

The fire of 1892 is the reason that the downtown architecture is so uniform. The harbour is small, the hillsides very steep, and 14,000 people were suddenly homeless, so everything was rebuilt at the same time and in the same style, with builders using the narrow, tall townhouse as a basic unit because of lack of space. Most houses were constructed well, but some were built hastily, with round wood and missing joists because of insufficient material. There was a lot of prefabrication with store-bought parts: the narrow clapboard, the window size, the trims. We tend to think it's associated with modern building, but it was quite common in those days.

In the past, the typical form of the Newfoundland house was clearly understood. The parlour was used for the Christmas tree and very special, and in some cases solemn, occasions—wakes and births. The kitchen was the centre: everything happened there. The whole social process inside the house and its relationship to the community were clearly defined and understood. Now the living pattern is more complex, and houses turn into hotel rooms.

Phillip Pratt, architect, St. John's

White bird

My father lived to be 92. He died eight years ago, and in later years, I used to spend a lot of time with him. He told me how, early in the century, a lot of the populace believed some people were witches who cast spells.

In 1903, a schooner was leaving for Labrador to get some seal in early spring. Many men from Change Islands wanted to go, but there weren't enough berths for all of them. Soon the schooner got stuck in the ice, near a place called Spotted Island. There was clear water outside the islands, and all the other boats were getting seals, but this schooner was stuck. One day, the mate said to the captain, "I wonder if that white bird that flies over every morning at 9 o'clock for the past three days has anything to do with this. If so, I'll fix it."

He got his gun, and he put the powder in first. Silver is one of the old European ways of dealing with people casting spells, so he cut up a silver coin and made some silver shot. When the bird flew over the next morning, he fired at him and hit him in the leg. The bird flew on, but the leg fell down. That day, the wind changed, the ice shifted and the schooner got out. They went farther north, got a load of seals and about two weeks later, arrived back to Change Islands.

People came out to see how they'd done, and they saw that they'd done well. But how was everybody here at home? Everyone is fine, people replied, except one woman, who fell and broke her leg. You see, her son was one of the young men who had wanted to go with them but couldn't.

I remember that old lady. People would say, "Don't offend her too much, she might cast a spell on you."

Canon George Earle, St. John's

John Priddle, François

Swearing

Father Laurie Locke came one time and announced he was going to stay overnight. I said to the girls, "Now we've got a priest in the house. Eight of us talking in our sleep, with the possibility of eight of us swearing in our sleep. Father Locke will never let me live it down, if I do it. The rest of you, he won't mind, but me? He'd torment me."

So I sat up in the rocking chair till 5 o'clock in the morning, and I wouldn't go to bed. Then at 5 o'clock, my son John rolled over in his bed and swore a big oath. I thought I'd pass out, so I crawled up the stairs quietly and went to bed. I remember nothing after that.

The next morning, Father got up. I came down, making out nothing had happened, and said, "How are you today, Father?"

"Well, " he said, "between the rooster crowing and the people snoring and you swearing, I've never heard anything like it in my life." And I wouldn't tell him I had stayed up all night so he wouldn't hear me swear. I never did tell him.

Rita Grant, homemaker, Corbin

Quinlans with totem pole, Conne River

Impenetrable forests

Newfoundland—I hate the place. I like tropical forests and heat and things that grow and animals that live. We practically open a bottle of champagne when we see anything alive that moves outside. The Newfoundlanders kill everything off.

Look at the vegetation. All these acres and acres of endless balsam firs and nasty spiky trees. We read about Newfoundland in South Africa before we came here. We read about Newfoundland's impenetrable forests. That sounded exciting; I like impenetrable forests. Of course, I hadn't realized what they meant. It is just like an assemblage of picket fences, all stuck together; it is impenetrable in that sort of way. All these silly little trees. There is no stature about the forest at all, and it is monotonously boring. It doesn't matter if one goes up the north side or the south side, east or west of the island, the vegetation barely changes.

If you go for a walk in the forest, you can be quite sure you'll run across an old car wreck or a deepfreeze or something stuck in the middle of the forest, rotting. The energy that has been expended on this island dumping huge bits of ironware in the middle of forests is unbelievable. If only they had devoted this energy to something purposeful, what a wonderful place they could have made of it.

They don't like this place; they hate this place. But they always sing. They are such dishonest people. They get so upset about ''come-from-aways,'' but the come-from-aways are the people who like this place. They are the ones who take trouble with it; Newfoundlanders couldn't care less. If they can get some money out of it, only then they love it. If they can cut down trees and get some money for them or dig a hole in the ground and get some money for it or pollute the place and get some money for doing that, that is all the land means to them.

There are wonderful opportunities in this country. I always felt the good thing about Newfoundland was that it wasn't so big you couldn't change it. It's only got half a million people, that's all. You could change things here.

But not a bit of it. You cannot change anything. They're as conservative as they come. They don't want anything better, they

Shoal Brook, Gros Morne

Peter Bell, Logy Bay

just want more of everything. The people who sit in the House of Assembly and the people who vote for the people who sit in the House of Assembly, they have no dreams about a better way of life.

Peter Bell, painter, Logy Bay

Young and didn't know the difference

I was out fishing days and days when I should not. That's what got me health in the condition I'm in today, three parts of it. If I had my days over again, I'd never have done it. It's all right when you're young, but when your age comes on, this stuff comes back to you.

Half what put my mother in bad health was I. I ought to have been in the house days and days and hours and hours when I was

Cutting out cod tongues, Bay de Verde

out on that water. I just shouldn't have been out on those days, the water rough, in one of them little open dories—cold, wet and hungry. I never got a thing out of it. I just had the urge that urged me on. But I puts my mother in trouble and me own self too. Young and didn't know the difference, that was the reasons. And didn't care.

After your age comes onto you, all this comes back to you. Days and days and days I've been caught having a cup of tea, and this will come to me, just the same as if I've done a crime. I'm sorry for it now, what I did when I was young.

Jobe Symes, retired fisherman, Port aux Basques

Seal flippers

Seal was declared to be a fish by the Roman Catholic Church, so the Catholics in Newfoundland were permitted to eat seal meat during Lent. It saved them from starvation at that awful period of the year, the spring.

Seal flippers are delicious. You have to take off all the fat with a razor blade, every bit. Otherwise, they are kind of bilious.

Now, the St. John's man has a very different-tasting flipper than the outport Newfoundlander. The St. John's man is used to not a well-rotted flipper but a "high" flipper, like a well-matured cheese or game that has been hung for a while. The flippers always came in on the big vessels. They'd been thrown in barrels on the deck or down below with a bit of ice shoved on top of them. By the time they came in, they were about three weeks old and often had a nice greenish tint, which would be scraped off carefully. The outport Newfoundlanders get fresh flippers, poor devils, and they have never tasted this well-matured delicacy.

The flipper is about 10 inches long. Some people like the toes; other people like the slightly higher part. Everyone to his taste. It is a very dark meat and very lean. We always have it simmered in a pan, with lots of gravy and sliced onions. It is served with potatoes and turnip and lots of lemon poured over it. You scarcely have to chew it.

Tender. Tender as tender can be. Tender beyond description.

George Story, professor of English, St. John's

Baie Verte

Resettlement

Joey Smallwood never had a book any deeper than what I had, I can tell you. But I'll never write a book.

I lived here in Corbin all my life. I'm 64. My mother died when I was 5 years old; she died with a baby. I don't even know what she looked like. I lived with my father. He was young then and a devil to drink. Booze—he used to want the booze all the time. My niece came to live with him, until she left and went with another man by the name of Stanley Brewer.

I went to work when I was 12 years old. I worked for $3 a month up in Little St. Lawrence. I done housework. I scrubbed on the board and put out the clothes. I used to have to lug water up a big hill from a brook. This was way back in the 1930s.

One day, I wanted to come home so desperately. I was pissed

off with it up there. The woman I worked for didn't appreciate what I done. It was a Friday. I got up in the morning, and the mine in St. Lawrence was just coming off shift. I looked through the window and saw my aunt and uncle coming into town: my mother's sister—Melinda Noolan, she was—and her husband, a crippled man by the name of Denny Noolan. "By damn," I said. "I'm going with ye anyhow."

I had to swim across the brook because there was no transportation. The ferryman wasn't up, and anyway, you had to pay him 25 cents. I didn't have 25 cents. I took me bit of clothes and put it in a paper bag, but the flops of the river took the bottom out of it, and I lost the little I had. I never had very much.

I stayed home then. I worked up here for Jack Grant. I reared all their kids before I got married. My husband used to work in the mines in St. Lawrence. He made good money.

My darling, if I was to tell you! He was blind for two years, my husband was. He sat there by the end of the kitchen table. I tended on him. He went to St. John's and had this cataract on his eyes took off. He sees pretty good now.

We moved to St. Lawrence in 1969. They told us the road to Corbin was going to be closed, and there was going to be no school. So we moved under the resettlement programme. We sold our home here and bought a house in St. Lawrence. In 1970, the youngsters came back here with their father for the salmon season. They loved being back. They didn't like St. Lawrence,

Mary Power, Corbin

so we all moved back. We sold our house, and we gave back the money to the government. We owns everything we have here.

I'll stay here for all the days I've got to live. I might go for the winter though. It was such a hard time last year—a real old-time winter. The snow was so high, I never thought I'd stand on grass anymore. But probably I won't go.

Mary Power, fisherman's wife, Corbin

Rocks for brains

The old-timers had it tough—but they did and they didn't. I was reading in *The Reader's Digest* just two nights ago about the acid rain, about 5,000,000 tons of sulphur going into the sky and falling on eastern Canada every year from the eastern States. I'm wondering. The beets didn't come up this year, and we've had an awful lot of southwest wind. That would bring the sulphur here. The old-timers never had those troubles.

This is getting serious, and people don't realize how serious it's going to be. One of these days, we're going to wake up and that grass won't grow. Fish won't grow. All the little rivers here, there won't be anything in them. What are we going to do then? If you start to think about it much, you'll go out of your mind.

Yes, people had it made back then. If they wanted a salmon, there were so many in my grandfather's time, you could walk across the river on their backs. There were oodles and oodles of them, but none now. If they wanted fish in the winter, they went down to the brook and cut a hole in the ice and speared eels. They had their own cows for milk and butter. They had their own sheep for wool, for knitting and weaving. There was always lots of grub, and they never had any worries about what they ate. If they killed a moose, they'd get Joe, Paul, Peter and Pat to help eat it in a week so it wouldn't spoil. They couldn't shove it in the deepfreeze, but they could always get another moose.

You have to look at what the purpose of life is. Were we placed here to invent equipment, put it on the earth and kind of abolish ourselves? That's what we are doing now. When the old-timers went out in the sea, everybody had his own little dory and each jigged his own fish. But now it is only two men on a dragger, and they bring all the fish in for everybody. The other fellows are sitting home, cursing and complaining about the system because they can't work. There's nothing for them to do. When you're working, you don't have time to complain. What do they want a man to do? Sit down, do nothing and let the equipment do all the work? I can't figure it out. I know when a man does nothing, he gets unhealthy.

There's a new water-treatment plant being built in Port aux Basques—a $3 million job. Last week, they were burning sheets

Fishing nets and floats

Spreading cod to dry, L'Anse aux Meadows

of plywood and 10- and 12-foot lengths of 2 by 4. There was nothing wrong with that wood. It had done its job, but the men weren't allowed to have it; they had to burn it. Isn't there something wrong with a society like that, with the scarcity of trees and the budworm killing it all?

We've got our world polluted by trying to make things easy for ourselves. Tractors and machines, they're all burning stuff up, polluting everything. I've used pyrethrins on turnip. I've gone out two days later, and the earthworms were as dead as wire nails on the ground. Then two or three days after that, I've found dead birds that ate those worms.

I don't know how long the earth will take to replenish itself after man has finished with it. That's what he's trying to do, finish with it, use it up. Man's first tools didn't pollute anything. I know myself this new equipment does—so we shouldn't have it. Any man who tells me we should has rocks for brains.

Leonard Downey, farmer, Doyles

Children's choir, Christmas Eve, François

Christmas past

You were asking about Christmas in François in my younger days. To tell the truth, there isn't much to tell about, as there were no trees decorated in people's homes. We ourselves never had a tree until after I was married, and I was 28 years old then.

We always celebrated the 12 days of Christmas, from the 25th of December until January 6th. Some of the customs were really old; the first pioneers who settled in François around 1850 were James Marsden, our great-grandfather, his wife and three children. He came from a little place in England, called Castle Cassia in them days. They might have changed the name by now, as no one can seem to find it on maps or in books.

There used to be a big cook-up every night of Christmas, starting late in the evening and ending in the early hours of the morning. Everyone in the place would have their turn, cooking something different every night. Most everyone had their own land meat they used to hunt from the hills. There were no deep-freezes or refrigerators, but when they got their meat in the fall and winter, they would clean it and hang it up in their sheds, what we call "stages." The meat would stay frozen for a long time, and when they wanted to cook something, they would cut off a piece the size they wanted to cook of whatever it was they had and let the rest stay until they needed it again.

There were no special places to dance in them days, only in people's houses. If there was going to be a dance, a couple of men would go around and ask the parents if their daughters could go to the dance that night. But no one was allowed to go to the dance, neither girl nor boy, until they were 16 years of age. And even then, one of the parents had to go with them to their first dance and bring them back home.

If a fellow liked a girl a little bit, he could never see her alone; the father was right behind them. He would have to kiss her in front of the parents or hold her hand or whatever. It might seem strange now, but it was their way of doing things then.

There was no music for years and years for dances, only one older man or a woman who would sit in the corner all night and sing jigs, while the crowd would dance to their tunes. The floors of some houses were pretty rough and hard to dance on. If a girl should wear a hole in the bottom of her boots on the dance floor, the next day, the fellow who asked her to the dance would have to put a new sole on her boot.

They always had their jars of rum, ready for anyone to have a drink as soon as they entered the house. But for years and years, there was no drinking from Christmas until Christmas again the next year. There was no electricity, no phones, no inside toilets, bathtubs or running water, such as there are today.

Times are different than in them days, but we were married 50 years ago last January, and we've managed to get through all these years.

I suppose we will manage the rest of our lives.

Joshua Marsden, retired fisherman, Louisbourg, Nova Scotia

Expensive stuff

I am always scared anywhere that's new. I am scared to go on the plane, scared on the boat. I get seasick, I get airsick. When we are taking off and landing, I always put my head down between my legs. When we are up in the air and it's bumpy, I get

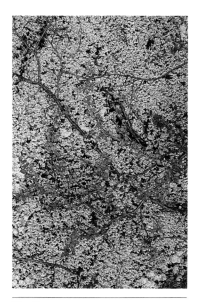

Caribou moss

sick in my stomach. I see stars, little old lights before my eyes.

I had to go to a meeting in Gander one time. We stopped at St. John's, where they told us the plane was delayed, so we sat around the airport. Then they said the plane was delayed again, so we went shopping.

I thought we would be going into a small store like here in Nain, but there was store after store, and I couldn't keep my eyes off the stuff. A store just for clothing, a store just for jewellery, a store just for music. I couldn't believe it. If those stores were in Nain, I think all the people would be in there all day long, looking. They'd never go out.

We went to a jewellery store and looked at some rings. We saw

Johanna Terriak and her aunt Miriam Brown, sewing sealskin boots, Nain

a ring with a little red stone on it, and we thought it would be about $190. When we asked the woman how much it was, she said $1,200. There was an alligator handbag for $249.

I kept wishing all these stores were in Nain. I liked looking at the vegetables and the fruit and the different kinds of meat most. They were all very fresh. Not rotten stuff like here.

Johanna Terriak, nurse's aide, Nain

I was the proudest damn father

"Twenty-one millionaires on Water Street got rich off the fishermen," Joey Smallwood said one time. He was right too. They couldn't contradict him. They took all our fish for nothing and got the biggest kind of money for it. Old John Crosbie, over at the House now, his father rogued the money out of me all his life. He's dead and gone, and what's the good of it to him now?

I had nothing—reared up poor right straight from the beginning. My father wasn't rich; he fished for work. He had no money. A lot of times, I had no money. But one of these days, I'll go to the same place all the millionaires have gone to and I'll be just as well off as them. I don't see what good it would be to me to try to haul the money out of you and rogue the money out of somebody else, then cram it into a box and shove it in the bank. By and by, I'm gone. The money is no good to me. Only someone else will row over it.

I've seen it done. A bit of money, $4,000 or $5,000, and they fight over that. Brothers and sisters. But I have none for anyone to row over; we always spend ours. There are people who never spend on their children and on their homes—they just cheek it— but ours is gone, all gone. We fed our children well, got them educated, all nine of them. We reared our garden with vegetables, raised sheep, caught fish, moose and rabbits in the woods. We had trout all winter long. We had it all. Every day I would sit down and put all my children alongside the table to pass out the food to them—pass a full plate to them. I was as happy as a lark then. I was the proudest damn father in the world.

Bill Pittman, retired fisherman, St. Pauls Inlet

no way. We were all poor, but it wasn't our fault. We were in one boat because we all had nothing. There was no jealousy.

I am proud about it, now that it's all over. The people seemed happier then. Today, they want to get what the other fellow has and a little more. It's not what you have, it's what you are satisfied with. Accept it. That's all that matters.

Paul Emberley, retired postmaster, Bay de Verde

The Pittmans, St. Pauls Inlet

Pennies

When I started working back in the 1930s, it used to cost two cents to post a letter, and sometimes people couldn't find two cents. There were no cheques coming in, only widow's allowance, $12 per quarter, $4 per month. They didn't live on it; they only survived.

One time when I was growing up, we were digging in a cabbage patch and dug up one cent—one penny. We thought we had a small fortune: we'd discovered a gold mine. We went to the shop and got a handful of candy, all for one penny. We made three piles out of them, for three of us.

Today, children get all kinds of money in their pockets. They have wallets. They go to the snack bar and get their hamburger, their chips, their pop, everything they want. We couldn't do that,

that you feel really alive. And the best part of it is being able to come back and tell about it.

I remember one time in a canoe, by myself. A hard wind came in from the east, up through Hebron Fiord. The waves whipped up high. Where should I go? There was nothing but bare rock on either side. All I could do was stay with it. If I'm to die up there, it will be the water. Or the wind.

Last year, we were flying by helicopter from Hebron Fiord across the Height of Land to Helen Falls to pick up the collars of some dead caribou and see what caused them to die. We had good visibility taking off, but the winds suddenly increased, and the weather came down. We were crossing the barren-ground

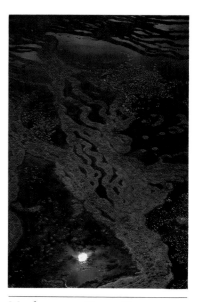

Muskeg near Goose Bay

The precipices of death

The Torngats are hard, hard mountains. They have a beauty that is unique, a certain starkness, ruggedness, bareness. A naked beauty, you might say. And they are tough. Having come from the West, I never thought there was anything in Labrador that could compete with the Rockies—until I saw the Torngats. Some of the experiences I have had up there have brought me the closest to the precipices of death. It's only when you walk along that narrow ledge and have a chance to look down into the jaws

Torngat Mountains

tundra with not a tree anywhere, not even a stick, only this howling gale. And we had to keep going into it.

We couldn't come down. The wind was blowing too hard, and it was too bouldery to land. We wanted to turn around, but we couldn't, because if we went any higher, we would've lost ground referencing and gone into a whiteout. So we had to keep flat to the ground, just crawling over the rocks. When we came to the top of one hill, I looked down and realized we were going backwards. We crawled carefully around that hill and managed to get into a valley.

We got the collars, but the pilot said he wasn't going to fly again and took a month off.

Stuart Luttich, provincial biologist, Goose Bay

During my first year in Nain, in 1959, everything was new. I spent a lot of time hunting, fishing and trying to do things the Inuit were doing. I asked a lot of questions, but everybody said, ''Don't ask questions. Watch what I do.''

The first caribou hunt I went on is particularly vivid. It was late in April. I went with Jerry Sillitt, who is now the head elder, Tom Barbour, Fred Atsetada and others. We went with dogs, crossing the neck of land north of Nain and into Webb Bay. We had heavy loads and had to get off the komatiks to help haul them up the hill. I jumped off, and the dogs started to race. Tom and I tried to leap on the komatik, but I knocked both of us off in a nice clumsy fashion. The komatik and the dogs went careering down the hill into a tree stump, the line broke, and the dogs disappeared off into the distance. We lost about an hour finding and untangling them.

On the second day, we went up a very steep gorge, from sea level to 2,200 feet in a very short distance. In some places, the dogs dropped in their tracks from sheer fatigue, while we all worked extremely hard shovelling away snow cornices to make a passage up through the gully. We finally got onto the Height of Land late in the evening and set up our tents. It was April, so it was too warm for snow houses.

The next day, we travelled on the Height of Land. The Inuit call it Sekuokak, meaning ''in the likeness of the sea ice.'' As far as the eye could see, the land was just white and—to me—flat, but the Inuit often had a name for a little hump. That day we made 30 miles. There were a lot of rock ptarmigan, and I'm told there were times when the Inuit were able to kill them with dog whips. We had .22s and shot enough for our evening meal.

On the third day, we encountered caribou—a small company of about 40 or 50. We anchored the dogs to keep them out of the action, and the men ran forward and got 15 animals. They didn't have scopes, only the old British .303s and 30-30s.

The next day was very hot. The sun was beating down and up at us, reflecting off the snow, and I felt as if I had a sunstroke. We were in rotten snow with about 1,800 pounds on each sled, and we really had to work. Finally, we came to a beautiful amphitheatre called Shiamonik—''the spreading-out place''— the headwaters of the Kingurutik River, leading off from the Height of Land down through a gorge and on to the coast. It was so warm; there was a nice, mossy area, already clear of snow. We stopped there and boiled up a big supper. It was a beautiful starlit night. We were so tired we decided not even to put our tents up and just lay down on the caribou skins in our sleeping bags. We got up at 3 o'clock in the morning to take advantage of the hard frozen snow before it melted.

We only made 12 miles that day, travelling from 4 o'clock in the morning till 11 o'clock at night. Hard work. We went through a narrow and bouldery gorge where the water was running so fast there was no ice. We had to take the dogs down the gorge one by one, cut grooves in the shore ice and haul our sleds on their sides just above this rushing water—very tricky, exact work because the sleds were so heavy. The Inuit didn't complain.

Fred Atsetada, who was alone on his sled, had dropped back a few hours earlier. We set up camp and waited. At 1 o'clock in the morning, Fred came around the bend, absolutely caked in ice, saying, ''The funniest joke happened to me around the corner back there. My sled went through the ice right into the river.'' He'd gone through hung-up ice into this fast-moving, freezing river, got his dogs out, unloaded his komatik onto the ice while standing in the water, then put his whole load back together. He thought that was just hilarious. I always think about him when I get caught in traffic and get frustrated by a few minutes' delay.

That attitude and sense of humour were symptomatic of the Inuit ability to survive in the North. There was also a tremendous bonding between people who struggled together in situations that, if you didn't cooperate, could be life-threatening. These people did it as a matter of course all their lives. That bonding was so strong that what I used to think of as serious disagreements were only superficial squabbles.

The people I was hunting with seemed to have had a total character change since leaving Nain. In the country, they were more alert and seemed to grow in stature. In Nain, they had been diminutive and argumentative; here, they acted like kings who knew what they were doing. They were more in harmony with themselves and their environment. You could see them just shining. They were happy.

Nain is an artificial environment. In the old days, people came there just to trade, to go to church and then return to their camps. Only when they started to live there for longer periods of time, with no real reason for being there, did the unhappiness, disagreements and alcohol abuse enter the picture. There is a tremendous contrast between people living fully and exercising their talents and those who are not. But how do you convey that to the people who live in the South?

Government planners tell the Inuit, ''You must live in a centralized community. Do this. Do that.'' But the Inuit can't relate to it. Theirs is an intrinsically cooperative society, while ours is a competitive one. In our lives, we don't cooperate with each other to succeed. We climb all over each other, don't we?

On day nine, we finally got to the salt water and the sea ice. Coming around Northern Point, we went into the belly-catters—the rafted ice above the rocks in the tidal zone—and up the slope to Nain. The whole village came rushing down and practically carried dogs, sleds and people up to their houses, helped them unload and asked how the hunt went. They were curious how I had managed. I had lost 15 pounds, and that night, I was ravenously hungry. And I was quite glad to have a bath.

Tony Williamson, international development director, St. John's

Signpost in Nain

Fishing on the Labrador

My father was a fisherman, and I married a fisherman—a true-born fisherman. Mike was 22 and I was 18 when we married. I had 13 children and raised 8.

Mike was 3 when he first went down to Labrador. He spent 67 summers there, never missed one. If he had a good summer, it was fine. If he didn't, he'd manage with it and go back again the next year.

In the early years, we'd go down by schooner. There was no engine into her, just the canvas. There'd be six other families. We'd go down in the spring of the year and often get caught in a jam of ice. We'd have to sit it out, until a fair wind came.

We took the pork, the corned beef and the flour, the molasses, the sugar, the beans, the peas, the hardbread, the prunes, the dried apples, the baking powder, the butter, a little bit of flavouring and a bit of icing for the cake. We took it all, packed in large barrels. I'd take a goat for the milk. I'd take 24 hens; that's what the men wanted—eggs. The baggage, the barrels and the nets were put down in the holds. You had six feet of space, so you put your sack, filled with shavings or straw, on the barrels and made up your bed with blankets and pillows. If you had children, well, they'd be around you.

Mike's fishing boat would carry six or seven men. Our boys started fishing when they were 14 or 15. They were men then, believe it or not. I used to go out onto the porch of our shack and see the boat coming in, right flat on the water, loaded full of fish. I often said, ''Now, thanks be to God. Look, ain't that a lovely thing to see.'' I'd be happy. The more fish you saw, the more you liked it. That was your dollar. No fish, no dollar. I used to go down on the flakes and cut fish throats. I cut 1,100 kentals of fish one year. A kental is 112 pounds. That's a lot of throat cutting.

Whatever I put before the men, they ate it. They'd get up and say, ''That was a wonderful meal, Mrs. O'Keefe.'' They loved the pudding and the fresh fish an' brewis. And the cod tongues— they loved the cod tongues. I'd cook fried salmon and molasses duffs. I'd take two cups of flour, a cup of raisins, half a cup of molasses, half a spoonful of bread soda and a spoonful of baking powder, a pinch of salt, a couple of tablespoons full of butter and

Mary Jo O'Keefe, Carbonear

Eclipse Harbour, Torngat Mountains, Labrador

an egg. Mix it up: keep it dry, not wet. Then boil it for two hours in a calico bag. When it comes out, it's right round. Perfect.

Every second day, I baked 13 loaves of bread. I did my washing on the board, bringing the water up from the brook. We had no television, no radio. There was no one else on the island to talk to, so we worked hard. Sometimes on a Sunday, Mike would take me out in the boat, just to have pity on me, I suppose, to give me a break. There was little freedom, but if you have your freedom, you can't have a family.

We'd return home to Newfoundland in the fall, and there was no one at our door looking for his money. We'd go to the post office, and there were no bills. What a pleasure.

Mary Jo O'Keefe, great-grandmother of 17, Carbonear

Cod catch, Bay de Verde, Conception Bay

What would I do in Toronto?

Conversations change with the seasons. In the summertime, it's the fishery. The men discuss the lack or abundance of fish, who is doing well and who isn't and where their cod traps are set. They discuss different boats, the nice shape of one or the sturdiness of another. In winter, we talk about the different ways of constructing cod traps. A trap is a "he"; there is no neuter gender in Newfoundland—everything is masculine or feminine. A cod trap has the traditional system of floats along the top, lead weights along the bottom and a carefully constructed twine box, about 45 to 50 fathoms round, hanging loosely in between. Making a cod trap takes a month and is tedious because everything has to be measured exactly.

In the spring, people gravitate to the water. The snow starts to melt, and one day, some guy will go down to the harbour with a paint can. A week later, someone will put out a herring net or a few lobster pots. Fishermen are the eternal optimists; we have to be. We're always going to catch more tomorrow than we did yesterday. But I wouldn't encourage anybody to go into fishing—it's too uncertain. I'm 40 years old, and I'm totally unskilled in anything except in what I do. What would I do in Toronto? At this point, I have no choice but to stay with it and take the good with the bad.

In the winter, I live on unemployment cheques, but I'm not ashamed of that. Here, if some guy is not on unemployment in the winter, people say, "What was he doing all summer? Why didn't he get enough stamps?"

This summer, my brother and I'll probably catch 100,000 pounds of codfish. That will create 50,000 pounds of fillets which, exported to the States, will bring $100,000 of new money into the country. But as a fisherman, I only get 6 percent of what the consumer in the States pays. I'll also work all winter, preparing my equipment to go fishing next summer. So when I get my unemployment insurance, I don't feel the government is giving me anything. If I was working at a salaried job for 12 months to bring that $100,000 into the country, I'd be considered a great guy.

Brian Walsh, mayor/fisherman, Bay de Verde

Fisherman, Bakers Brook Cove

I work for social services, helping families. When there is trouble, I come and talk to them, maybe to the wife, if there is violence. Sometimes women come at 2 o'clock in the morning, scared. They have no place to go. It is hard to get women to talk: they don't want to admit what's happening. Sometimes I have to visit a few times. I know there is trouble, I just don't know what it is, so I keep coming, hoping they will tell me.

One woman told me, little by little. Her boyfriend used to get her drunk, bring his friends, make her go to bed with them. She has seven children, no place to go. She was scared to leave, so scared she sometimes would drink with him, just not to be afraid. After she told me, I sent her to a house in town and then started to look for an empty house in Happy Valley where she could move to. But she didn't want to leave here and came back. She neglected her children, so finally the kids were taken away from her. Now she is drinking too.

If only there were more people who would help and do what I do. But it seems there are just a few of us who are trying to do everything, and we just can't.

Yesterday, I ran for the band council. I got 87 votes. That's a lot, and I didn't pay for them. Some others would promise, "Vote for me. I will buy you some beer." But I didn't. I don't want to buy any votes. I told people, "Vote for me as I am." And they did, but not enough. I wasn't elected. I want women to run, to be on the council. I tell them to run. They say, "No. I can't do public speaking." I couldn't either, but when you have to, you do. Now I can—I speak to anybody. I run also to show other women that

Rose Gregoire, counsellor, Sheshatsheits

they can do it too. But even yesterday's election was a bad time. Drinking, before and after.

Alcohol ruins people here. It causes all the problems. People drink, get in trouble, drink some more. I said to others, "I don't drink, and you don't have to drink either." I went to Goose Bay, got two VCR tapes and two packs of cards with my own money. I told the people, "I will keep the Alcohol and Drug Abuse Centre open"; they can come, have coffee or tea, play cards. We can watch films instead of drinking. Some came—10, maybe 12.

But last night, I worried. My daughter—she is 11—didn't come home. Somebody told me he saw her drinking beer with some guys. I didn't know where to look for her. Finally, she came back. I tried to smell booze on her breath but couldn't; she went straight to bed. This morning, I said to her, "Tell me the truth. I won't hit you." She said, "Mama, you promise you won't hit me?" and she told me she had a couple of cans of beer. I called the RCMP and told them these guys were giving my 11-year-old daughter beer. The RCMP promised to find and apprehend them and call me back. I'm still waiting.

Rose Gregoire, counsellor, Sheshatsheits

I had never seen anything so vast and open and free before I saw Labrador. Britain is like a giant garden, very beautiful, but it is a garden. Labrador is the real thing. It is relatively untouched yet, and you can see things as they should be, without man's interference. Living here, I have a sense of being part of the natural whole.

To truly see, there has to be a spring-cleaning of one's inner self. Then one can see not only the total picture, which is magnificent, but also the very minute things. I remember walking one hot evening. The flies were terrible. I squatted down, looking at some flowers, and I heard this crunching sound. As I turned my head, I saw a dragonfly eating a large bush fly, and I could actually hear the crunch as it was being eaten. It was fascinating, and I wondered how many other people had watched a dragonfly eating a fly and actually heard it.

Red-tipped pudicularis

My first close encounter with a bear was another of those special moments. There was a slight hill with a large rock on top, and all around the rock were good berries. I'd seen moose and bear tracks, so I knew animals were around. I longed to see something. I approached the rock, and about 30 feet away, there was Mr. Bear feeding on berries. My first thought was, "What a magnificent coat." The sun was shining, and his fur was the most beautiful shimmering brown. Then I felt fear. I stood watching for a moment, turned slowly around and started walking away. Suddenly, I thought, "What am I doing walking away? All these years, I have been longing to see this." I cautiously approached the rock again and peered over the top. The bear was standing on his hind legs, looking directly at me. It was his berry patch, and I was the intruder. I turned around and walked away. I didn't get my berries there that day.

I was given a rifle as a gift. I liked eating the partridges people gave me, but I felt I should take the full step and supply my own needs. A great deal of soul-searching went into my first shot. I

Hockey, François

Mischief

Us young fellows loved playing hockey. We had an outdoor rink, and the ice was good, but we didn't get out of school till it was almost dark. We figured the only way we could get a bit of time to play was to do something with the school furnace, so we threw water in the tank. It was a cold night, and all the lines in the school froze up. The furnace backfired and blew smoke up through the ducts. It went everywhere. The classrooms were full of soot. They were a week trying to clean it up. We got dismissed from school for a while, but we didn't mind.

John Grunter, lighthouse keeper, Greenspond

Cats, François

Mummering, François

Mummers

At Christmas, we go mummering. Men puts on women's clothes, and women, men's clothes. Sometimes, you puts on old rubber clothes that you went fishing in. This year, I had on a woman's outfit, a skirt and what they call a nightdress—I had on one of them. A few of us got together, and we went all around the harbour. We were into Aubrey Greene's, and his brother got the accordion out and we cracked her down and did a nice bit of dancing. Nobody could guess who we were. We had on the real store-bought false faces. When you put on one of them, it's not very often anybody knows you. I had on a false face that looked like a young person, sort of like a doll. Some of them were real *h'ugly*-looking ones, men's faces.

There's times when they can tell you by your movements. You've got to try and act like another guy when you're dressed up, to fool everyone. You can take a drink if you want one, but lots of times you won't, 'cause they'll catch on if they see your hands or something. You have to lift up whatever you have on your face before you can drink, and people try to sneak a look.

Harvey Baggs, fisherman, François

Hanging fire

I came to Twillingate on a boat. The captain and I were trying to converse, but he didn't understand me, and I didn't understand him. I went below to sleep. Then two shots rang out. I looked out, and there were two turrs dead in the water. Now, in Ireland where I come from, nobody shoots a seabird, and nobody would dream of eating it.

Well, my captain was fishing the birds out with a dipping net, so I asked him, "What did you do that for?" He said, "Good to *h'eat.*" "Oh, heat, heat—of course," I said. Oily bird—they must extract the oil for heat, very clever, very smart, that justifies it. But I learned they ate seabirds. I said, "My God, I couldn't dream of eating one." About a week later, I was invited for Sunday dinner, and my host told me, "You'll never guess what we're going to have for dinner. A great Newfoundland delicacy, turr!" I got to like it. Now I'd walk from here to Twillingate for another turr.

They'd been using muzzle-loading shotguns in those days. I had one myself, but I gave it up after I saw people coming to the clinic with powder burns. Sometimes in Twillingate, this big flock of turrs or ducks would come down. First, you would see the smoke of all the muzzle-loaders, then hear the shots all the way down the shore—shot, shot, shot—from all the boats. Some people would knock off a dozen birds with one shot. But it was

Grouse hunter

a dangerous business, too, because some shotguns would not go off. They called it "hanging fire." They couldn't hold it in hand all day, so they would tie the stock of the gun to the boat with a rope so that when the gun eventually went off and jumped out of the boat, they could haul it back in.

Michael Maguire, dentist, St. John's

138

Lobster Cove Head

Bull-bird

The little bull-bird, that's a fantastic little bird. It comes in the early winter. There are little ears on it, and they stick up like the horns on a bull. That is why this town came to be called "the bay of bulls" by the French.

On the way to school, I'd go down by the mouth of the river, and the little bull-birds would come in on the smooth water. I'd go out—and probably get my feet wet—and grab one right quick and put it in my pocket. Then I'd go on to school. I'd keep it in my pocket till 3 o'clock in the evening, hoping it wouldn't bawl or squeal and the teacher wouldn't hear it.

The nuns were pretty strict with us, and if they heard a bull-bird in our pocket, we had to go out in front of everybody. We'd bawl and cry, and the nuns would make us go down to the sea again and put it right back in the water.

Joseph O'Brien, retired fisherman, Bay Bulls

Strip-mined

Newfoundland has always been strip-mined in every sense: by the glaciers, which caused the absence of soil nearly everywhere; by paper companies; and by the domestic use of forests. It was strip-mined of its marine resources—take it, take it all out, don't even bother to put anything back.

This snatch-and-run reflex is very characteristic of Newfoundlanders because survival here is so marginal. You get your hands on something and hide it like a dog hiding a bone. Do it before somebody learns you have it and takes it from you.

People make money in Newfoundland and buy real estate in Florida. They don't trust anything here. That's another removal without replacement. We also lose an immense number of able people. That's true of Nova Scotia too, but the farther you are from a sponge such as New York or California, the more you are going to lose.

It's very difficult to convince Newfoundlanders to relinquish something today on the grounds that it may multiply tomorrow. In Churchill Falls, we learned what Confederation was going to be all about. The way our Churchill Falls energy was sold in Quebec taught us about the total disregard for equality and fairness in the Canadian political system; it has to do with numbers, as any democracy does.

We didn't even have the option of selling our electricity to New York. We had to sell it to Quebec. But if Quebec had had an immense resource and Newfoundland sat between this resource and its logical market, there wouldn't have been a question about transmission lines across Newfoundland. We would have just said, ''Yes, sir, thank you, sir,'' and been grateful to get jobs putting up wire poles, which would have marched right across us without any questions whatsoever.

To me, this was an illustration that in Canada, the strong would not be fair to the weak. That the weak would remain weak and that the strong would rule. And that is the way Canada is run. Newfoundland is the weakest. We are thrown bones and told, ''Bury this, bury that.'' But at what point is weakness cowardice, and at what point is it simply a result of having been crushed and humiliated by a succession of people from outside?

Log booms, Deer Lake

century is a story of populations seceding from major confederations, of Pakistanis trying to get out of India, of Quebec trying to get out of Canada. But Newfoundland looked around to join someone else. Such humiliating behaviour is not supposed to happen in the 20th century.

Humiliation has a backlash. Newfoundlanders give an impression of meekness and sweetness to people who come here from outside, but they don't exhibit it to each other. If you have something that an average Newfoundlander doesn't have, it's a source of bitterness. If you sail your boat into one of the small communities and you have the Stars and Stripes on the back of it, everybody there is as sweet as can be. But if you have St. John's, Newfoundland, written on it, then it's automatically assumed you have robbed fishermen for three generations. A lot of animosity is directed against those who might be getting ahead of other people. And generations of our politicians have preyed upon it, cleverly using this sense of bitterness to their own advantage.

Christopher Pratt, painter, Salmonier

The presence of American bases emasculated us. About 30,000 Newfoundland girls married American servicemen, who had money in their pockets, who could buy liquors and cars, who had their own teeth. That meant there were as many Newfoundland guys who had to stand there and watch it happen.

The British maintained a colonial rule here, yet in 1932, we voluntarily surrendered our own administration and asked the British to come back and run us. The world's history of this

141

Inuit men gathering firewood near Nain

Slave mentality

Somebody asked me once why I thought people drink so much, and I said, "Slave mentality."

How do you help people who think they have no choice but drink because their lives are controlled by the government? The government says, "I don't want you to do that. Do this." But what can we do? We have to have a permit to get firewood. We can't go anywhere now with a gun in our hands. We have to have a gun licence. Even berries—we can only pick them at certain times.

In the spring, I went out caribou hunting. They put me in jail for that, but I'm not going to stop for them or for the department of wildlife or for the government. According to my culture, I didn't do anything wrong. That's the way I was brought up, the way I live. They think we should be able to adapt to their culture easily. We can't. We also don't want to lose our culture.

You don't want anybody telling you what to do. You don't want anybody telling you what way you should live. If we do everything the white people say, then we are just as crazy as they are.

Julianna Pasteen, former social worker, Sheshatsheits

Christa, Sheshatsheits

Ornery society

This is not a society as painted by the tourists who talk about the Newfoundland warmth and love of strangers. This is a very cantankerous, ornery society, but with a continuity to it and a toughness to it. It's not a glad-handing society. It has a strong awareness of the "come-from-away" people and is reluctant to pull strangers in. Newfoundlanders have a particular sense of self, and it takes a certain effort to break through that reserve, that wall. If you are just passing through, you might do it easier. It is not an unfriendly society, but it's somewhat fearful of strangers and therefore protective. You have to earn that trust. George Story, who wrote the *Newfoundland English Dictionary*, says that the continuity of this very ornery society, which insists on being itself, is amazing.

In the outports, where the ordinary fisherman's family was

Louise Belbin, Grand Bank

functionally illiterate, some people lacked self-confidence and were cap in hand, beholden to the merchant. But that was a specific situation, a different sense of culture. I don't think Newfoundlanders trust people. If they see them as having power and this great god of education—such as an Anglican minister or a Catholic priest or the RCMP or the welfare officer or a merchant—they may fear them and therefore defer to what they say. But it doesn't mean they trust them.

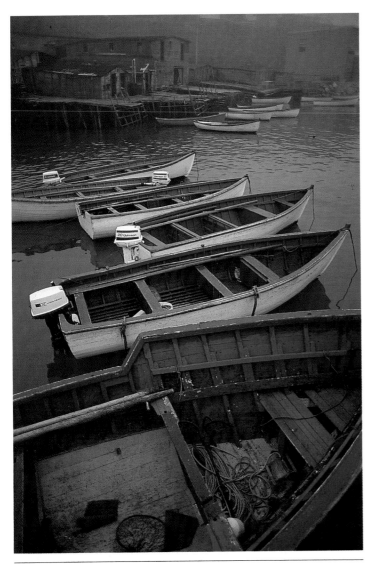
Harbour, Bay de Verde, Conception Bay

Yet there doesn't seem to be much duplicity here; you know clearly where you stand. People are not hypocritical. If they don't like you, they'll make it clear, and when they do, they'll make that clear too. That's what makes politics so exciting in this province. You can see wheels within the wheels. People get nasty with each other, but it's all up-front, in full view. They are not afraid to argue and have enemies. It's an entertainment, something everybody is involved in. If you ask an average Canadian who his Member of Parliament is, he might not even know. Here, they do. It makes it much livelier.

It's not a polite society, but it's an honest society. Yet there is a real reluctance toward confrontation. If I lived in a small village and wanted to borrow your boat, I wouldn't come to you and say, "May I borrow your boat?"—forcing you to say yes or no. But I would start chatting with you, talking about the weather and the sea and the state of fish, and in the course of a rather long conversation, you would know that I would like to borrow your boat. And you would just as indirectly let me know whether I could borrow it or not. And neither of us would have lost any dignity in the process.

Tony Williamson, international development director, St. John's

145

The ice receded from the coast of Labrador around 9,000 years ago, and the first people came in, spreading up the coast. They moved their camps to be at certain places at certain times of the year, and the animals came to them. It was a matter of timing and knowing nature extremely well: the caribou migration, salmon migration, seal migration. The harp seal population was fabulous, and when they were pupping on the pack ice and the ice came close to land, these hunters must have had a bonanza.

But if you missed the migrations, the place where the caribou crossed the river or where they went through a certain pass or if the pack ice stayed well offshore, then you missed the boat entirely. Your stock of skins, of antler, of meat, of sinew and of fat for that coming winter was gone. You might get by with one miss, so if the salmon didn't come, you could still live on seal and caribou, but if you had major problems for a year or two, that would be it. That would be the end of the entire local population. That's perhaps why you find mass extinctions, where a whole people just disappear from the archaeological record.

So the same type of cycle went on for thousands of years. The stronger, more vibrant people would come into an area, armed with new technology and better able to exploit the resources, and the resident population would just fade away. The Maritime Archaic people were replaced by the pre-Dorset Eskimo, the pre-Dorset Eskimo by the Dorset Eskimo, and the Thule Eskimo replaced the Dorsets.

Shuldham Island in Saglek Bay was a perfect location for a spring camp. We know from our findings that Dorset Eskimo people camped there, and later, there were Thule and Labrador Eskimo. Perhaps there were some early Maritime Archaic Indians long before them. All these people would have had the resources of the ice edge and of the ice itself: polar bears, seals, whales, walrus and land mammals—caribou, fox, black bear.

The early Dorsets built semi-subterranean house pits at the Shuldham Island site. Only two or three families camped together, and some of the dwellings were large enough to house two families. It is a beautiful site, with everything they needed: sod for building the house walls, flat stones for making sleeping-platform bases, fresh water from the pond, shelter from the north and east, a good view out of the bay. We found tools made from Ramah chert, which is a coarse-grained, translucent stone used for making cutting, scraping and hunting tools, and there were all sizes of soapstone pots and lamps, from large to very miniaturized, that might have been playthings used by kids to emulate their parents' activities. There were also small soapstone carvings of humans, bears, seals, whales and other beings. Some might have been used by shamans to ward off evil spirits, to gain the aid of helping spirits or to attract desirable things. When you carve a figure of a polar bear, you might be trying to gain some of the latent spiritual power the polar bear has.

One tiny soapstone carving of a human figure at the Shuldham Island site has a deep gash in its back, a short hooded jacket and the traces of boots. The figure, if you look at it from different angles, could be swimming or flying or just sitting with its back arched—or stabbed . . . a whole number of things you can read into it. There are no Dorset people to ask what it meant. You can just imagine the wild stories of violence and sexual exploits and of the exciting lives these people must have had.

We know that even 6,000 years ago, the Maritime Archaic Indians knew of the Ramah chert resources just north of Shuldham Island. But artifacts made of this chert have been found as far away as Ontario and Maine, which is exciting because it could only have gotten there by being traded from hand to hand.

Shuldham Island is such a beautiful place to do archaeological work. It's so wild. You can leave your tent's flaps open and hear the waves crashing on the beach and see the northern lights and hear the silence. At the same time, you worry about your boat moored offshore and wonder about your progress on the next day. Then you get up in the morning, start to work and peel back these layers. You go back through time, finding tools you didn't think would be there.

Why? What are Point Revenge Indian arrowheads or spearheads doing at Saglek Bay, in northern Labrador? Did these Indians come north to extract the Ramah chert that they were so fond of using? Or were these tools given in trade to Dorset Eskimo who had brought the chert south to the Point Revenge Indians? Or were these two arrowheads or spearheads impaled in the butts of two Dorset Eskimo who had made it back to their camp and then died there? How did these points get to Shuldham Island?

One summer, we were walking on a caribou trail in the interior of Saglek fiord. We stumbled across a gravesite that had been cleared out and made into a hunting blind, and just on the other side of the caribou trail, there was this tiny cache, about two feet square. And inside the cache, there were layers and layers of Inuit grave goods: spearheads, harpoon heads, scrapers, ulu blades. And right among these tools, there were some Dorset artifacts.

That was fascinating. Everybody who works in this field is looking for the connection between the Dorset and Thule people. In Labrador, the Dorset period existed much longer than elsewhere in the Arctic, so you have greater potential for contact. And here, in this gravesite, were several Dorset cutting tools made of green nephrite, very finely polished. Was it a Dorset man who took a Thule wife or vice versa? Or were there two families living together, contributing their respective tools? The grave was typical Thule, with a broad vista over the sea, facing south to get the maximum sun. There must have been some trade of knowledge; the Thule didn't know where the slate outcrops were that they could have used for their tools, and perhaps the Dorset people were able to tell them. Also, the Thule didn't know where the soapstone was for making their pots and lamps, but the Dorset already did.

Once, we found a soapstone carving, less than a cubic inch in size. Two people entwined in an embrace. You can't quite figure out their position; they are either head to head or head to tail. They both appear to be naked. Again, you can speculate: Were they both Thule, or was one a Dorset person? Were they two males or two females or one of each? Was this a meeting of the two cultures and the way of assimilating? Or was it a wish on the part of the resident Dorset to be able to do away with the problem of the incoming Thule? What were they doing on that long winter night? We may never know, but we keep on trying.

Callum Thomson, archaeologist, St. John's

Archaeological dig, Shuldham Island

Laying the keel

The older people have always said, "You don't build boats—they grow."

Newfoundlanders start from scratch. The wood is collected from the hills, brought out, sawed, dressed and shaped into various pieces. The plan comes from a small hand-carved half-model, because boats are symmetrical. The whole process is indigenous to Newfoundland, from the idea to the finished product. It's hard physical work, but there's a special pleasure gained from putting in place pieces of organic material to form a boat, a tremendous satisfaction that craftsmen find in working with their hands over the years. It's really an art.

There are different ways to build boats. One is scientific, as in marine or naval architecture, where the problem is attacked by working with figures and specifications and you're able to say why you're doing something a certain way. The other, the way old people have learnt from their forefathers, is by feel and by eye. If they want the boat to look a certain way, they'll look for a tree with just the right shape for the stem. They set the keel, scarf the stem to it and rabbit in the stern post. That's how a boat begins.

When we were building our sailboat, I asked Gordon Pittman, the old boat builder I work for, where he thought the waterline should go. He stood back, and I went up to the stem with my pencil and put a mark on it. He said, "Raise it up a couple of inches." I did, and we walked to the stern.

"Yes, that's it, about there," he said.

"Now, where do you think we should put the mast?" I asked.

He stood back again, looked at the boat and said, "Right there." I put a mark on the rail, squared it across, and that's where the mast went.

When you do it that way, you may not be developing quite as efficient a boat as someone who does it with all the calculations, but your boat is very functional.

It works, and it's seaworthy, and that's the ultimate.

Gary Pittman, boat builder/community liaison, Rocky Harbour

Gordon Pittman, boat builder, Rocky Harbour

There were 11 dories to a schooner, two men per dory, a deck-hand, the cook and the skipper—25 men. We'd take our frozen bait out of storage and leave for the Grand Banks in the spring of the year. We had wooden tags with different points written on them: north, south, east-by-north and so on. We'd put our hand in a small bag and draw one out. We'd row out on that course and set our lines. There were 50 fathoms on a line, 10 lines in a tub and usually 5 tubs in a dory.

We'd start at the crack of dawn and make three runs a day. We often got 150 kentals between us. There's 112 pounds in a kental. If we got a deckload of fish, it would be 1 or 2 o'clock in the night before we got it all split. We'd only get a couple of hours' sleep that night. You can't go very long like that.

Up on the south coast, around Rose Blanche, we'd set out in the morning with torches, machines with a big wick and full of oil, something like a burner. We'd catch that afire, and it'd give us light to set our gear by. The dories weren't too far apart, so if you got into trouble, you'd stick your oar up and the fellow next door would come over. If the schooner had her flag up, that meant "come on aboard," 'cause the wind was going to beat up.

The dories would often run astray from the ship. Sometimes, the ship would heave up her anchor to go look for them, and the dorymen would be looking for her, and perhaps they'd gone one way and she'd gone the other. A lot of dories got cut down by large ships. We had three of them cut down—run into in the black thick of fog. I don't suppose that those ships ever knew they'd struck anybody.

We got about $150 for the year, March through to November. The merchants owned and outfitted the schooners. You didn't see much bacon and eggs, I can tell you. Around Christmas, they'd settle accounts. If we had something coming to us, well,

Moored fishing boats, Bay de Verde, Conception Bay

all right; if we didn't, same thing. We had to do it to get something to eat—work daylight to dark.

There was no good way to feel about it or say, ''I'm going to jack the price up and go on strike,'' like they do today. For the men on draggers now, it's a picnic. They're the old-age-pensioners crowd. There's no work to it.

John Douglas, retired doryman, Grand Bank

Living here

Only those who lived here can tell you what it really was like. People who come from away say to us, ''You must have felt so isolated.'' How could we have felt isolated when we were living at home? When I go to different places in Canada and the States, then I really feel cut off from the world.

We spent the summers on Duntlin Island. The island was 12 miles out from Cartwright, a mile or so from Packs Harbour. There were three families there, three little red houses. I knew every rock on that island. When people came to visit, we showed them everything, but if there were birds' nests with eggs in them and we didn't think the kids that had come to visit were sensitive enough, we wouldn't take them near those.

The mice would chew up the fishing gear, so we would go on mouse hunts. We would get big long sticks, follow the mouse trails and kill as many as we could. But we made darn sure we

Sunrise over pack ice, Labrador Sea

were never near the two graves when it was dark. It is a spooky feeling when you walk past a graveyard at night, the same as when you walk past an empty house.

We didn't have much. My father just made enough for us to live from day to day. In Cartwright, we always felt a bit inferior, not quite as good as the people who lived up the harbour, but on Duntlin Island, everybody was the same.

One summer—I think I was 15—I got to work with the fishing crew. My Uncle Jack got sick, and they needed someone to work on the stage. I heard my Dad ask Mum, "How do you think Doris would work out cutting throats?" Mum said, "Well, why don't you ask her?" So he asked me, "Do you want to help us at the fish today? If you're any good, we'll keep you on." I went down, and he showed me what to do. I thought, "I'm going to keep up to the old man, or he's going to say I'm not good enough." That night, I heard him tell my mum, "She's as good as any boy in the darn place and better than most." I was all right.

The next year, Dad asked if I wanted my own salmon net. I sure did. He only came home on Saturdays, so he asked my uncle to put it out for me. I waited nearly all week, but he just never got around to it. So I said to Mum one day, "I'm going to put it out myself." All the shore-fasts were out and the lead ropes, so I just had to row the net out there, tie it on and put out one grapelin.

That Saturday, I saw Dad's boat coming, and I was so proud; I was going to tell him I put the net out myself, but he got to Mum first. I heard him ask if my uncle did it, and Mum said, "No, Doris had to put it out herself."

"Oh, my God!" he said. "I'd better go and tighten the knots." He went straight over, and when he came back, he said, "I couldn't have done better myself."

When the time came to take the net up, I had to haul out the grapelin, and that was the only thing I couldn't do. I would get it up to the stern, but every time I tried to tip it in, the boat took water. I couldn't swim, so I thought I'd better leave it. I felt such a failure. I had to row home and ask Dad to go out.

"That's all right, my mate," he said. "I'll get it."

And he did.

Doris Saunders, editor of Them Days *magazine, Happy Valley*

Tablelands

The Tablelands, in Gros Morne National Park, is a large chunk of the earth's mantle that broke loose. It was thrust up from several miles below the ocean floor and heaved sideways on top of the crust, the layer we live on. The part of the mantle that was deepest inside the earth is now near Bonne Bay. The bit that butted against the underside of the crust is near Trout River, where one can clearly see the transition between the red Tablelands rock and the grey gabbro of the crust's bottom layer.

Surrounded by green mountains, the Tablelands are a rust-red, bare massif. Surprisingly, there are some tough and very specialized plants that like the chemistry they find on this huge hunk of rock, which really belongs deep inside the earth.

Those that like it, love it. There is thrift, one of my favourites, very common in Europe but not in North America. It belongs to the carnation family and has a lovely pink head about the size of the ball of your thumb. There are also moss campions, beautiful, smooth green pincushions with tiny pink stars, neatly filling the crevices between the rocks.

The dwarf rhododendron bushes, also growing in the Arctic and through Siberia, bloom in June, and that is when one suddenly recognizes them. There are bluebells that find life in the gritty eroded pockets. Their flowers form great drifts of blue.

Where you hear water tinkling underneath the rocks, you will find pitcher plants. Normally, you cannot see their beauty because they grow in a bog surrounded by grasses, but here you can kneel beside them.

On the Tablelands, every flower, however tiny, stands out. Some of them are absolutely minute, but you notice them because they are not competing with other vegetation. Many are so unusual for this part of the world that you won't find them in the North American flower books. You are left wondering, "How did they get there?"

The Tablelands is a place to study rocks; but to me, it is also a place to botanize.

Pat McLeod, artisan/writer, Curzon Point

Tablelands, Gros Morne

Shoreline, Southeast Arm, Bonne Bay, Gros Morne National Park

the outside. If there is a light in the kitchen, it is time for their evening cup of tea, and I am familiar with that ritual.

It is not nosiness. It is a feeling of belonging and having all kinds of rights to do this. In some instances, when I know there is an older person living alone, it is almost a duty. I certainly wonder if the light is out earlier than usual or left on later than usual. The next day, I make a point of finding out if there is something wrong. Not directly, because if you ask direct questions, you alarm people, but there are ways.

Gisela Westphalen, physiotherapist/artisan, Curzon Point

Lights

Our nearest neighbour said again and again, ''Your light is company. I never go to bed without first looking across. When I see your light, I know we have neighbours again.'' I found it beautiful, but it was foreign to me. Having always lived in cities, I enjoyed the darkness.

After many years of living in this village, I now understand what a light in a house means. I know the families and their houses, their kitchens, their porches. When I walk through the village at night, I know this light is in the living room, that one in the bedroom. Passing the houses is like visiting neighbours. Some are watching television: one can see that very clearly from

François

Petitions

Outsiders see Newfoundland as an impoverished, barren land where things must be simple. Yet they are not. They are very complex, and you miss or misunderstand everything that is going on till you start to see a special level of sophistication.

A few years ago, a local entrepreneur wanted to build a video arcade here. There was a great deal of opposition in the community. City council didn't know what to do and recommended gathering names of who was "for" and who was "against." So two opposing camps went out with their petitions, collected a weighty number of names and duly presented them to the city council. The town councillors were impressed with the size of the two petitions. But when they started comparing them, they discovered that the same people were on both lists. How exquisitely Newfoundland it is, that whoever approaches you, you will sign whatever he presents, just to be pleasant and diplomatic. Unlike in most civilizations, where there is a winner and a loser, where somebody walks away from social encounters bleeding and wounded, here, both people emerge as winners. This kind of system has a crazy side to it, because so much of social reality gets pushed into a corner, but it accords a level of respect to everybody, and I can't think of many other places that do it so well.

I love it here. If I ever have to leave, I will go sobbing and screaming.

Elliott Leyton, writer/anthropologist, Torbay

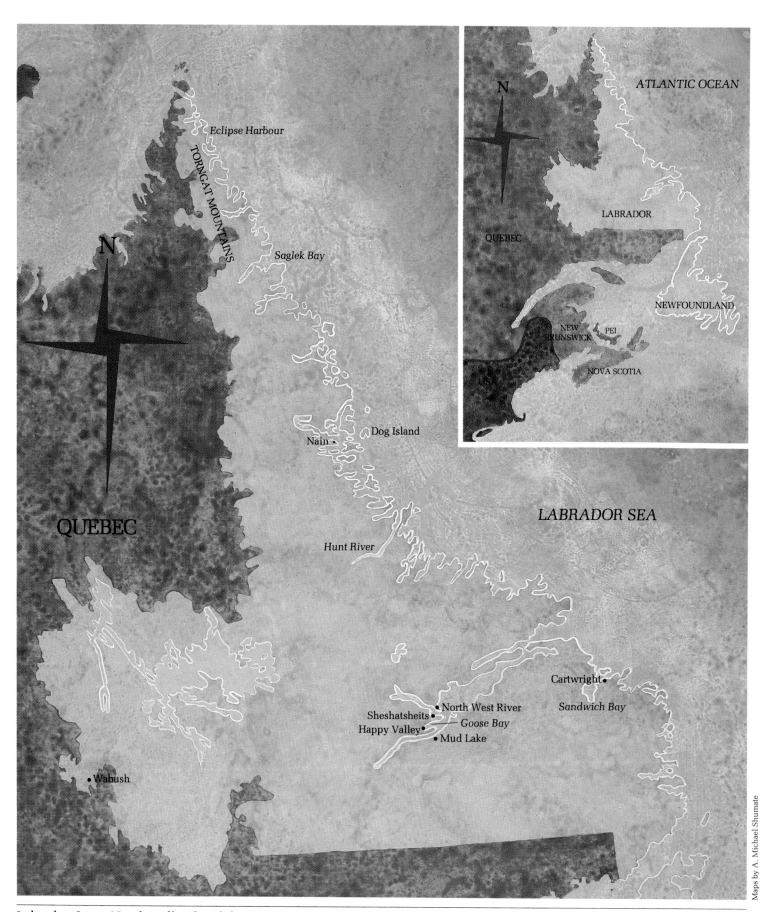

Labrador. Inset, Newfoundland and the Maritime Provinces

Maps by A. Michael Shumate

158

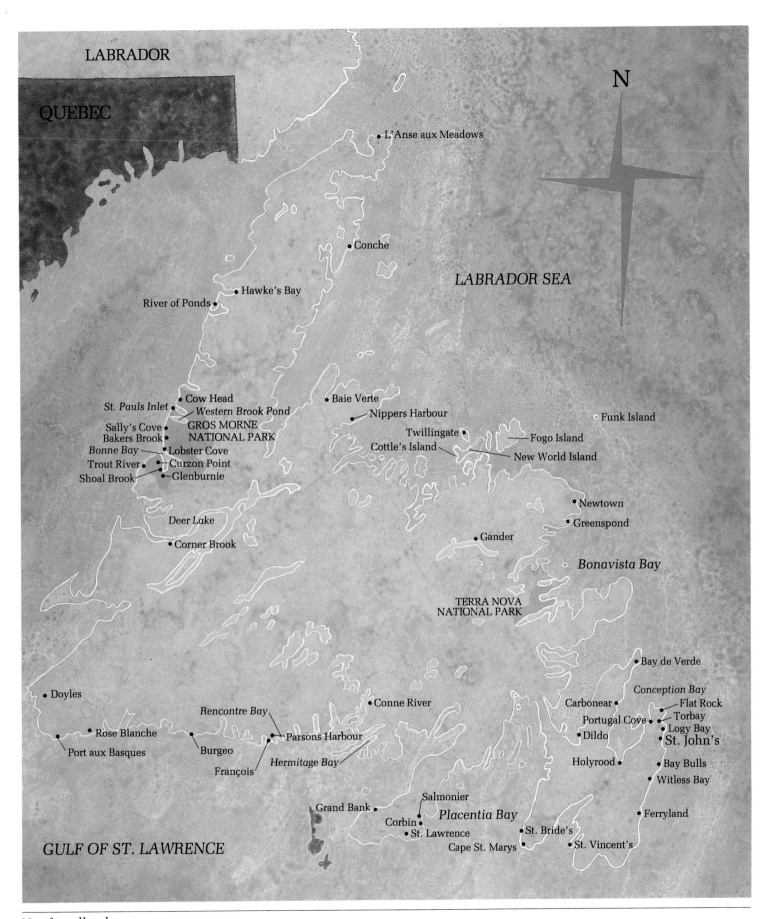

LABRADOR

QUEBEC

N

• L'Anse aux Meadows

• Conche

LABRADOR SEA

• Hawke's Bay
River of Ponds •

• Cow Head
St. Pauls Inlet •
Western Brook Pond
Sally's Cove •
Bakers Brook •
GROS MORNE
NATIONAL PARK
Bonne Bay
• Lobster Cove
Trout River •
Curzon Point
Shoal Brook
• Glenburnie

• Baie Verte
Nippers Harbour •
Twillingate •
Cottle's Island
Fogo Island
New World Island

• Funk Island

Deer Lake

• Corner Brook

• Newtown
• Greenspond

• Gander

Bonavista Bay

TERRA NOVA
NATIONAL PARK

• Bay de Verde

Conception Bay

• Doyles

• Conne River

Rencontre Bay
• Rose Blanche
Parsons Harbour •
Burgeo •
Hermitage Bay
Port aux Basques
François •

Carbonear •
Portugal Cove •
• Dildo
Flat Rock
Torbay
• Logy Bay
St. John's

Holyrood •
• Bay Bulls
• Witless Bay

Salmonier
Grand Bank •
Placentia Bay
Corbin •
• St. Lawrence
Cape St. Marys
• St. Bride's
• St. Vincent's
• Ferryland

GULF OF ST. LAWRENCE

Newfoundland

159